What makes contemporarauthor's crisp
expertly balai
with hilarious passages that delve into such topics as
buying food in bulk and her late-night internet
addiction....An insightful, honest, and genuinely funny
author delivers a standout devotional.
- *Kirkus Reviews*

When she was a guest on the Focus on the Family
Broadcast, Shannon Guerra shared a wonderful message
with our listeners about the power of adoption. *Oh My
Soul* is an encouraging and uplifting chronicle of how
prayer has helped sustain her through the joys and trials
of family life.
 - **Jim Daly**, President, Focus on the Family

It's been a long time since a book has set me ablaze like
this one! Shannon uses the interesting layers of her life
in Alaska to paint pictures from her experience about the
practice of prayer and how to carry God's presence.
From the clever title to the very last paragraph, I
consumed this entire book in one sitting! Everyone who
is serious about knowing God should pick it up!
- **Dr. Chuck Balsamo**, Pastor, Author, Pro Speaker
and Coach

In *Oh My Soul*, Shannon takes your hand like a dear
friend, offers you a cup of tea, and walks through your
daily life with gentle reminders of the Father's great
interest and constant involvement in your life. She's real.
 She's raw. Life's messy. Her fresh approach to praying
without ceasing will forever change the way you pray, the
ways you love others, and even the ways you trip over
your kids...and your cats.
- **Dr. DiAnna Wallace**, N.D.

Prayer is an often overlooked practice in the midst of our busy, messy lives and Shannon is here to remind us that prayer can join us in our mess and be a lifeline between us and God no matter the circumstance. Her honesty, humor, and wisdom shines throughout *Oh My Soul*, and helps us all learn to pray from a place of victory.
- **Amanda Bacon**, The Masterpiece Mom
TheMasterpieceMom.com

Paul's encouragement to pray continually wasn't meant to be a line item on a religious checklist. Shannon's vulnerability, honesty, and humor give a glimpse into the messy reality of a mature Christian's prayer life — the imperfectly perfect ongoing conversation and relationship between a child of God and her Father. This book will encourage and comfort you as it gently breaks down any walls of duty or sterile piety in your heart and mind toward prayer.
- **Nathan & Lacey Steel**, Directors of Cultivate
CultivateDiscipleship.com

Only read this book if you are prepared to be inspired, admonished, and encouraged. *Oh My Soul* is beautifully prophetic, reminding us that God's voice is speaking, right now, right here, in the middle of the mundane. With her trademark humor and lyrical writing style, Shannon invites you to shake the dust off your Bible, find a posture of prayer, and start living as the warrior you were created to be.
- **Natasha Metzler**, Author of *Pain Redeemed*

I'm not just being kind when I say I loved this book. So much of it resonates with where I've been, where I'm at, and where I'm headed.
- **Lenora Brake**, Brake Ministries International

With fearless vulnerability, this work shows us what it means to wrestle and, win or lose, emerge stronger and wiser. Grappling with God and family, with authors, Scripture, and her own weakness, the insights Shannon shares will refresh and encourage anyone who has tackled the awkward project of "praying without ceasing."
- **Luke Epperson**, Pastor & Director of Operations
Church on the Rock
Wasilla, Alaska

Simply put: Shannon has written a book every disciple (follower) of Jesus should read, because it captures real life in Jesus, guided by the Holy Spirit, to get to know the heart of a loving Father God. Read this book - and learn what it means to be (and *become*) the real you in Jesus. Jesus changes everything, and hearing Him is the key to this relationship.
- **Scott Frerking**, Lead Pastor
Hill Country Fellowship
Burnet, Texas

What a beautiful, practical book on prayer and what it looks like to meet God in every detail of our day. I was either laughing or crying from how the Holy Spirit spoke to me as I read it. Such powerful truths about intimacy with the Father and being real with Him that I can relate to.
- **Sarah Frerking**, Director of Women's Ministries
Hill Country Fellowship
Burnet, Texas

Shannon is a master wordsmith, weaving her everyday tales to lead us all to the heart of God using the language of the human soul.
- **Elizabeth Gilroy**, Founding Director
Face of Justice Association
San Jose, Costa Rica

Also by Shannon Guerra

Upside Down:
Understanding and Supporting Attachment in Adoptive Families

Oh My Soul Companion Journal

Oh My Soul Devotional:
21-Day Complete Study
3-Day Mini Studies

the Work That God Sees series:
Prayerful Motherhood
in the Midst of the Overwhelm
Capable
Allied
Growing
Steadfast
Resilient
Seen

oh my soul

ENCOUNTERING GOD
IN HONEST,
UNCONVENTIONAL
(AND SOMETIMES MESSY)
PRAYER

shannon guerra

ISBN 978-1-7325719-3-8
ISBN 978-1-7325719-4-5 (hc)
Library of Congress Control Number 2018910463

Scripture quotations are from the ESV® Bible (The Holy Bible, English Standard Version®), copyright © 2001 by Crossway, a publishing ministry of Good News Publishers. Used by permission. All rights reserved.

Portions of scripture in **bold** are the author's emphasis.

Cover art by Kelly Bermudez, Willow Lief Design Co.
Author photo by LaCroix Photography

This title may be purchased in bulk for educational or group study use. For more information, please email shop@copperlightwood.com.

Printed and bound in the United States of America

Published by Copperlight Wood
P.O. Box 870697
Wasilla, AK   99687

www.copperlightwood.com

For Vin,

my behind-the-scenes hero

...UNTIL THE SPIRIT IS POURED UPON US FROM ON HIGH,

AND THE WILDERNESS BECOMES A FRUITFUL FIELD,
AND THE FRUITFUL FIELD IS DEEMED A FOREST.

THEN JUSTICE WILL DWELL IN THE WILDERNESS,
AND RIGHTEOUSNESS ABIDE IN THE FRUITFUL FIELD.

AND THE EFFECT OF RIGHTEOUSNESS WILL BE PEACE,
AND THE RESULT OF RIGHTEOUSNESS, QUIETNESS AND TRUST FOREVER.

MY PEOPLE WILL ABIDE IN A PEACEFUL HABITATION,
IN SECURE DWELLINGS, AND IN QUIET RESTING PLACES.

- ISAIAH 32:15-18

Contents

abiding:

HE IS THE GOD WITH US

For God alone, O my soul, wait in silence,
for my hope is in Him.

Psalm 62:5

The sun rises here long before we awake. The light is streaming, the shadows shrinking, and kids are stirring. This is just the beginning –

– because later, the cat is throwing up and the tea kettle is squealing and the phone is ringing and the kids are running and three children are calling for mommy when someone knocks on the front door asking if we want our carpet cleaned. And we do, but not this second, and not by a solicitor who wants an audience.

Sometimes it's everything at once, and other times it's just one thing at a time.

Either way, I'm learning this in both the quiet and the chaos:

> *The time of business does not with me differ from the time of prayer; and in the noise and clutter of my kitchen, while several persons are at the same time calling for different things, I possess God in as great tranquility as if I were upon my knees at the Blessed Sacrament.*
>
> *- Brother Lawrence [1]*

I'm practicing, and getting better.

Afton asks about volcanoes, and I draw eruptions and the sedimentary layers of lava flow on the back of a Costco receipt...and He's here.

Nerf darts fly over my head and hit my leg as I type in the middle of the crossfire, and He's here.

I see a puddle of cat puke on the dining room floor...except it's dripping from the bench...that a child is sitting on...and I realize, *oh, expletive,* it's not cat puke at all but an entirely different kind of volcanic explosion. I stand there stupefied, wondering what to do first.

And it takes me a few minutes before I realize that He's here with me, too, lifting me to a new level of motherhood, because I survived (and cleaned) a poop-tastrophe of such magnitude that I briefly considered just buying a new house.

I cleaned the floor and the bench and the skin – the child's, and yes, mine, too – and the clothes and everything and everywhere else.

He was right there, the whole time.

He is no less with us in the chaos than the calm, but sometimes we listen better when it's quiet. Sometimes we even hear Him better in our dreams, in our sleep, in our dormancy. We lay ourselves down and we hear what we would not listen to in our waking hours.

Our arguments, frustrations of the day, and backburner worries are either buried or resurfaced as we sleep. He's still there with comfort, with answers, with rest. If we ask, He'll tell us things that dispel every shadow we have long feared. He will show us how to clean the mess.

And in the morning, He'll be there long before we awake. The light will stream in, and it will be just the beginning.

During fall in our corner of Alaska, the leaves crackle when you step on them, but it's not like the thick, potato-chip crunch of fallen leaves in the lower 48. It's a thin, smashy sound like walking on wrinkled tissue paper, mostly birch leaves. Light sparkles on dying fern. And on wet and spongy days, when rain drizzles the afternoon away and the teapot hums continuously, water condenses on the windowpanes.

At the end of September I walked in fertile ground, picking up scraps of thoughts and themes He kept laying out for me. I set them aside for temporary storage to pull from in the October evenings, as you might stock your pantry with favorite canned goods, preserves, and boxes of tea.

It wasn't the first time. For two years in a row, I'd asked God to teach me how to pray without ceasing.

> **In all circumstances** take up the shield of faith, with which you can extinguish all the flaming darts of the evil one; and take the helmet of salvation, and the sword of the Spirit, which is the word of God, **praying at all times in the Spirit,** with all prayer and supplication. To that end **keep alert with all perseverance,** making supplication for all the saints.
>
> – Ephesians 6:16-18

You can file it under either "the abundantly generous nature of God" or "be careful what you ask for" – take your pick – because in spite of only asking Him about unceasing prayer, He was aggravatingly thorough. He insisted on teaching me about grit, surrender, confession, repentance, fear, brokenness, friendship, shame, procrastination, hope, identity, routine, and healing.

Mostly, it was just Him and me talking in the off moments. I need to hear His thoughts in normal days, in grey days, in dark days, to steward my life well.

We're still talking. I'm still learning.

I'm convinced that learning to hear Him changes everything. Disasters averted, hearts healed, people saved, dreams realized. Missions accomplished.

And you and I, we're here walking through all of our days, partnering with Him in ways that bring life and make the darkness flee. Outwardly, we're on our feet, eyes open – inwardly, we're on our knees, eyes up.

You tell me nothing new: you are not the only one troubled with wandering thoughts. Our mind is extremely roving; but as the will is mistress of all our faculties, she must recall them, and carry them to God as their last end.

– Brother Lawrence [2]

On the eve of launching a blog series about praying without ceasing, Vince found me sitting on the couch puttering around with a photo editing program. I confessed I was redoing all of my graphics because it was the most productive way to procrastinate I could think of, and he left me there cropping photos while he went upstairs to tuck in the kids.

By the time he came back downstairs, I had two satisfactory images. Then we prayed like we always do in the evening, but I interrupted our conversation with God three times to talk about writing, collaborating with a friend, and our dire need to trim the cats' claws sometime in the next few days.

When we were done, I faced the computer squarely. This was it. No more stalling. I inserted the new graphics into the post and proceeded to methodically type out "day 1," "day 2," "day 3," and on and on, which was a wonderful, non-thinking autopilot activity until I got to day 31. And then there was nothing left to do, but...write.

And I did – for about 98 words, until I got stuck trying to figure out an illustration. I needed some ideas, some inspiration. And right then, wouldn't you know, I hit on the perfect solution. *I had to check Pinterest.*

It was all in the name of research, of course. Thanks to my commitment to learning about prayer, I'd hardly even peeked at the opiates – I mean, opportunities – on there.

I knew I should be writing, or doing the dishes, or at the very least, getting the cat off the counter where she was hunting for leftover scraps of dinner, but there might...be something amazing...if I scrolled...a little farther...

BAM. A recipe for one of my favorite cookies that uses only three ingredients. Told you.

Charles Spurgeon once said, *The worst thing that can happen to a gambler is to win,* and he's

right, because upon further investigation I discovered that one of the "ingredients" was a com-
mercially-made cookie consisting of 38 chemicals
that looked similar to what I've seen on labels of
laundry detergent. So it wasn't a win for me; it was
a disappointment.

What did you expect? the Spirit asked.

Well, with only three ingredients...I guess I was
hoping for a miracle.

*Well, Love, you were looking in the wrong
place for that, weren't you?* Did you know the
Spirit will sass you back sometimes?

I moved on, and after forty-five minutes I
finally figured out what I needed for the illustration, which seems like an unimpressive return
on my investment. But I also pinned six things,
read three articles, and firmly rejected the idea of
painting all of the doors in our house aqua.

Maybe you've noticed. There's only one difficulty with the concept of unceasing prayer: the
"unceasing" part. We humans are highly distractible.

> *I believe one remedy for this is to confess
> our faults and to humble ourselves before
> God. I do not advise you to use multiplicity
> of words in prayer, many words and long
> discourses being often the occasions of
> wandering....If [your mind] sometimes
> wanders and withdraws itself from Him,
> do not much disquiet yourself for that;
> trouble and disquiet serve rather to dis-
> tract the mind than to recollect it; the will
> must bring it back in tranquility.*
>
> *– Brother Lawrence* [3]

Sometimes we err in thinking that prayer needs to be refined, holy-sounding, and set aside for remote, quiet places where no one goes – like the woods, or, let's be honest, a neighborhood HOA meeting – with faint strains of classical music in the background.

But, no. Nope, not at all.

Prayer needs to be right here with us in the joy and mess of everyday life because this is where we need Him: in these moments of office meetings, running errands, helping customers and coworkers, scrubbing stained carpet, and teaching our kids math (especially that). Our conversation with God is constantly interrupted, and yet, not so – because He's right there, unoffended by the activity of daily life.

It's not just our distractible nature that is roving. He is moving among us as we go about the hours of our day.

Hey, Love, He said, *when you're bored and scrolling without purpose, looking for inspiration and not finding it, it's time to look in a different direction.*

When you're overwhelmed and looking for distraction and escape, look for Me instead. I have wonderful things to distract you with, and I will help you find your focus again.

Your time with Me will never disappoint you. I will always leave you wiser, or rested, or both.

You don't want to miss this.

This time with Me is bountiful, potent, and effective to change and restore anything you are avoiding. This time is fertile to bring forth what you are awaiting. This time creates prolific momentum toward everything you are working for.

This time with Me is never a gamble.

You will always gain. You will always bear fruit. You will always find peace when you find Me. You will always win when you spend time with Me.

Our awareness of His presence allows Him to come between us and our agendas, and He is with us at the desk with our computers, at the table with our kids, and with us when we sleep. His peace is for you, for me, every second.

Day 1. Day 2. Day 3. He's right here with us, and He's in all the spaces between, too.

It's the middle of the night, and I'm slowly brought to wakefulness by something. I lay there for a minute in the haze and listen.

There it goes again.

Dripping. Not rain, though.

Something different, and the effort to ignore it only makes me more awake. I roll out of bed and find the source – the shower head is still running in a drizzle, even though it's turned off. *Weird.*

I turn it on a little and then shut it off again, and it eventually stops. It's 4am and I fall back into bed wide awake. Now my brain is dripping even though it's supposed to be turned off, and I've had two hours of sleep.

So I start to pray. God plays this trick on me often, and I know it's not just me because many of you have told me He does the same thing to you. He wakes us up in the middle of the night – or, He lets something wake us up in the middle of the night – because someone needs prayer, right then, for that moment, for the day ahead, or for the day they just struggled through.

I pray randomly at first, just general things: our country, our government, our kids, our town. It's not long before He brings something specific to mind.

But then I stall, hesitating – and because I am selfless and sacrificial, I tell Him, "God, I don't want to pray for that. It will just frustrate me, and I'm trying to get back to sleep."

And lightning doesn't strike me.

Instead, He says, *That's because you're doing it wrong, Love.*

Oh.

And because He is (really) selfless and sacrificial (and also, not tired) He explains it to me.

You've forgotten to pray from victory to victory, He says.

You go from glory to glory, even if the middle place is frustrating, because then you can pray from joy.

You can pray from a place of victory to a new place of even greater victory because I've already won.

And then we pray, from joy. **Hope comes.** Mountains move, the dripping stops, and I fall back to sleep.

All around me, the leaves are fluttering, the puddles are drying, and the kids are sliding down the stairs in a sleeping bag because they're thrill seekers who are tired of waiting for snow and winter and proper sledding.

Elsewhere, the news is blaring, the government is stalling, the people are asking, and the buck is passing. We need answers, peace for this moment right here, right now.

He has a word for you and for me, for this time. He has the answer in this moment. Let's wait for it.

Ready?

Go.

Aaaand, crickets. I hear nothing.

Often when I sit down to write, it takes a long time for words to come. I'll get up, clip my nails, get more tea, pet the cat, sit back down at the desk... then I'll get up again, walk to the bathroom, straighten the counter, sit back down. It's practically aerobic.

So much of writing is just thinking and waiting for words. It doesn't look very productive. It's still work, but it feels like running in place. I feel like I'm stewing, or stalling, but I'm really just percolating. You know, like coffee.

Hearing God is sometimes like this. He speaks, but for me to hear Him, all of the distractions have to be filtered through so His words can permeate. I have to percolate for a while.

He's not stalling; He's not wringing His hands. He's waiting, too.

I'm not being patient for Him. *He's being patient with me.* He knows that I can be a slow learner sometimes. And also, a little attention deficit.

If it seems like He's stalling when we're trying to listen, it's for the best of reasons. When we have questions and the answers don't come immediately, the pressure we feel is probably not from Him in the first place – it's from the beast looking for a willing victim.

The distractions and pressure are bait. Resist them, and starve the beast.

The answer might be simply to wait. Hold on. Hug the kids. Find that coffee. His words will come, so just sit with Him. The longer we soak, the stronger we get.

There is no work in life so hard as waiting, and yet I say wait...All motion is more easy than calm waiting. So many of My followers have marred their work and hindered the progress of My Kingdom by activity. [4]

Some things you just can't rush, like listening to God, raising children, and healing from trauma. And don't forget teaching arithmetic, which some of us might consider a combination of all three.

There's a child in our dining room sobbing over math, over eight times four. But it's okay, I've got this – step aside, folks, stand back – I'm no rookie, I've done this before:

"Make it smaller," I tell him. "What is eight times two?"

"Sixteen." *Sniff.*

"Great! Now, what is sixteen times two?" I check to make sure my super hero cape is ruffling in the wind, like it's supposed to in the movies.

"Thirty-two...oh!" He writes down the answer, and I think he's got it figured out – until ten seconds later, and he's sobbing again. Nine times four, good grief.

We try it again. "What is nine times two?" And then, thinking of a new strategy, I ask him, "If eight times four is thirty-two, what is nine times four? What is four more added to—"

"*WAIT!*" he interrupts, trying to think. He's already on the trail, but my chatter is in the way. "Thirty-six!" he yells, victorious.

It reminds me of that scene in *Finding Nemo*. *Let us see what Squirt does, flying solo...*

When we get to the point of truly waiting – we've listened, we've obeyed, we've taken the leap – it's hard not to interfere. I want to hurry things along; I want to read too much into the situation. I want to yell at God for being a Big Meanie. It's like peeking at the popcorn while it is popping, though – at best, we delay what we're already waiting for, but at worst, it blows up in our face.

> *For in this hope we were saved. Now hope*
> *that is seen is not hope. For who hopes for*
> *what he sees? But if we hope for what we*
> *do not see, we wait for it with patience.*
>
> *– Romans 8:24-25*

And so I'm learning to wait. Apparently He thinks I need lots of practice at this.

The next time someone sobbed over multiplication, I was prepping dinner. We really need to enforce the "math before mental shutdown" rule.

"Mom, can I get the abacus?"

"Nope, you can do this." *Let us see what Squirt does, flying solo...* A few minutes passed, sprinkled with wailing and moaning while I sautéd onions.

"Mo-*oooo*-om, can I get the abacus?" I hope you're reading this in the whiniest font imaginable.

"I already said no." *Wait, and be not afraid...* and I'm praying in the moment, but these poor onions. They don't deserve what I'm doing to them at this point.

"Mom, can I get the abacus?" And, hey, I didn't answer him again. See? This is me, waiting. This is me, not interfering. This is me, not letting my chatter get in the way. *Patient Mommy... gooood Mommy...*

"Why can't I use the abacus?"

And then, it must be confessed, I flung the hero cape to the ground. Patient Mommy was done.

"Because I am a BIG MEANIE."

See? I told you I need lots of practice.

Ezekiel. The judgment of Tyre.

This is what I'm reading in the Bible today, and I would nod off except that I know this filling from the Word needs to happen before I tackle any of the billion projects and chores on my list.

And, I'm sorry Ezekiel, but the judgment of Tyre doesn't seem to be speaking into any of them.

I consider reading faster. Skimming. Skipping. Trying a different chapter.

Come in anticipation, He says, *not compulsion or religious duty. Expect something. You don't need to do anything faster.*

I protest. This chapter doesn't apply to anything I'm dealing with right now.

Read anyway, He says. *Don't miss this.*

My eyes are on the page as I continue reading, but my mind is clearly on the day and the tasks ahead of me. Suddenly, thoughts are brewing. Ideas and solutions are coming like they hadn't before. I'm distracted, but somehow...productive.

You're not distracted, He says. *You're yielded. This is a powerfully effective position to hear from Me, and I have all the answers you need.*

Your obedience to read My word steadfastly, not wavering or in fickle randomness, puts you in a posture to listen.

Spirit and truth collides. I'm getting answers for the day, and my mile-long to-do list is already simplified. I'm only halfway through the chapter.

Well, are we done now? I ask Him.

Is that all you want? He says, and I can hear Him smiling. *Do you want to settle, or do you want more?*

Oh. There's more? When You put it that way... okay, let's finish.

In my striving for productivity, for efficiency, for increased ability in these rapidly widening tent pegs, I'd gone about it wrong side up. I don't know how He does it; I just know that there's nothing in God's word that says "blah, blah, blah" – so instead of skipping over the sticky pages, He's taught me to listen for Him to speak.

It's not about speed, He says. *You can't follow Me faster.*

It's about devotion, which cultivates abund-ance.

But seek first the kingdom of God and his righteousness, and all these things will be added to you.

- Matthew 6:33

When you are devotedly pursuing Me, your capacity turns exponential. Grace never adds up correctly. Grace multiplies.

Rummaging through the kitchen, through cabinets, the lazy Susan, the pantry. Looking for tea, knowing we're out of the kind I like, but checking to see if any has magically appeared in the last twenty minutes anyway.

Vince heats up leftovers while I putter around him, shuffling things around.

"Fiending?" he asks. "Craving sugar?"

"No, procrastinating." I start pulling things out of the spice shelf. "I have no idea what I'm writing about tonight. Didn't we used to have a jar of tea here somewhere? You know, a jar –" I make hand motions relative to the size of the jar I'm looking for "– that's glass? A glass jar?" You can tell I get really stupid when I'm low on caffeine and high on filibuster.

"Loose leaf?" he asks.

The man is so patient. He knows I'm not really looking for tea.

"No, tea bags...in a jar...that one." He pulls it down from the top shelf and hands it to me, and I check the contents. Sure enough, it's full of eight years' worth of rejected tea bags, which is why they were stuffed in the back where I can't reach. No matter how hard I try, I can't make myself like green tea.

I hand it back and sit down, tea-less, to stare at a blank page. This is how it goes some days. I type and delete, I consider ideas and reject them – too personal, too boring, too repetitive, too much me. I get tired of hearing my own voice and seeing my own words; the rut is a deep groove that runs in a circle. I'm praying the same things over and over and it feels like I'm getting nowhere.

So I go back to finding His voice, and just read.

I will extol you, my God and King, and
bless your name forever and ever.

Every day I will bless you and praise your
name forever and ever.

Our kids memorized this entire psalm over the summer, because I'm a pitiless taskmaster and assign fun projects like that.

Great is the Lord, and greatly to be
praised, and his greatness is unsearchable.

The words are familiar and my eyes start to glaze over, so I read aloud – it's still my voice, but they're His words, and they start to merge onto the same track again.

One generation shall commend your works
to another, and shall declare your mighty

acts.

*On the glorious splendor of your majesty,
and on your wondrous works, I will med-
itate.*

*They shall **speak** of the might of your
awesome deeds, and I will **declare** your
greatness.*

I picked this psalm for the kids to memorize
because there was so much about words in it —
words spoken, words aloud.

*They shall **pour forth** the fame of your
abundant goodness and shall **sing aloud**
of your righteousness.*

*The Lord is gracious and merciful, slow to
anger and abounding in steadfast love.*

*The Lord is good to all, and his mercy is
over all that he has made.*

And as I'm reading aloud, my thoughts move
upward and out of the rut, and He's bringing to
mind those who don't have the Word, those who
can't read the Word, and those who won't read the
Word.

*All your works shall **give thanks** to you,
O Lord, and all your saints shall **bless**
you!*

*They shall speak of the glory of your king-
dom and tell of your power,*

to make known to the children of man your

*mighty deeds, and the glorious splendor of
your kingdom.*

*Your kingdom is an everlasting kingdom,
and your dominion endures throughout all
generations.*

He brings the most amazing thought as I'm
reading aloud. I start thinking of believers in prison, persecuted, and He tells me to ask for them to
be able to hear me, to hear His words. I believe He
can do this for the grieving in the quiet and chaos of
a prison cell.

*The Lord is faithful in all his words and
kind in all his works.*

*The Lord upholds all who are falling and
raises up all who are bowed down.*

*The eyes of all look to you, and you give
them their food in due season.*

I ask Him to let those who are persecuted and
fleeing hear His words in their running – in their
minds, in their hearts, in their language. He can do
this in the desert, on a mountain, in a hiding place,
anywhere.

*You open your hand; you satisfy the de-
sire of every living thing.*

*The Lord is righteous in all his ways and
kind in all his works.*

*The Lord is near to all who call on him, to
all who call on him in truth.*

I ask Him to let those who lead hear His words in their waking and in their sleep, whether they want to or not. I'm asking Him to make them hear His voice in their heads until they merge onto His track. He can do this in the White House, on Capitol Hill, in Parliament, and in our courts.

> *He fulfills the desire of those who fear him;*
> *he also hears their cry and saves them.*
>
> *The Lord preserves all who love him,*
> *but all the wicked he will destroy.*
>
> *My mouth will speak the praise of the Lord, and let all flesh bless his holy name forever and ever.*
>
> *- Psalm 145*

He sets to rights what was missing before, and the wheels turn on a path that has direction again.

identity:

KNOWING WHO

WE'RE DEALING WITH

It's a stage we all go through; it takes a certain amount of living to strike the strange balance between the two errors either of regarding ourselves as unforgivable or as not needing forgiveness.

Madeleine L'Engle [1]

She sits at the table, watching others play, learn, and go about their day. Just sits there, for hours.

She knows exactly what to do to join them and play; she needs to be excused from the table, and she knows exactly what to say to be excused. There was a time when she didn't know, but that was a year ago when she first joined our family after surviving years of neglect and trauma in a foreign country. On this day, she sits, choosing to do absolutely nothing rather than move forward, interspersed with occasionally trying inappropriate ways to leave the table. She's been through the full repertoire. Testing, testing, one-two-three.

So she sits and fights the inner struggle. It's hard on mama, too, and I struggle and pray.

Why is simple obedience so hard?

Shame, fear, and control are merciless taskmasters. Remember?

Oh, yes. I remember. A friend and I talked about it in depth a few months ago. I sat in the passenger seat of her car while it idled in the driveway and hastily scribbled what He was telling me:

People are afraid of changing because they fear future shame, not understanding there is no shame in repentance. It's the enemy's ruse to keep them from growing closer to Me.

They only need to ask to be excused, and My grace covers them.

We see the same thing in forming attachment. This daughter and another son of ours lived in institutions until they were almost seven years old, and they learned that adults are not people to get close to – so now, they have a hard time trusting me and my husband. They fight and test in ridiculous ways. It's a ploy from the enemy to keep them from growing closer to us, as well.

Because healing comes in the closeness.

The prodigal wonders, *If I change now, will I be ashamed and embarrassed later of who I was, when who I am now becomes who I used to be?*

I was there. I remember.

But He says, *There's grace for imperfection. I have a pardon all ready for you.*

To the one fighting shame and fear and control – and those are the same things, really – He says, *I know you're not perfect. I know you need growth.*

I know your past, your upbringing, and the indignities you've suffered and inflicted.

I know.

> *As to going home, shame opposed the best motions that offered to my thoughts...from whence I have since often observed, how incongruous and irrational the common temper of mankind is, especially of youth, to that reason which ought to guide them in such cases...*
>
> *...They are not ashamed to sin, and yet are ashamed to repent; not ashamed of the action for which they ought justly to be esteemed fools, but are ashamed of the returning, which can only make them be esteemed wise men.*
>
> *- Daniel Defoe* [2]

He says, *I still want you closer. No shame, no fear, no stumbling.*

Back in the dining room, this little girl has sat at the table pretty much all day long. It's bedtime now. I prayed, encouraged, stood firm, smiled, hugged, and pictured the victory all day, and now I'm out of ideas. "What do I do now? God, what should I do?"

Ask her. Just ask her what she should do.

I sit down with her at the table. And I ask her, not just once, but continually, because this is how her conversations go:

"Reagan, what should you do?"

"Um...bedtime?"

"Yes. What should you do for bedtime?"

"Um...brush teeth?"

"Yes. What should you do to brush teeth?"

"Um...upstairs?" (You see how this goes?)

"What do you need to do to go upstairs?" and finally we get there:

"Umm...be excused?"

"Yes!" *Stay calm, mama.* "What should you do to be excused?"

And we've finally arrived at the point.

Excused (adjective): absolved, exonerated, pardoned, discharged, freed, reprieved, released, vindicated, acquitted, spared, forgiven

Forgiven.

Every time she's tried it the wrong way, it hasn't worked out for her. Maybe it's time to try obeying and see how that turns out.

"Excuse me, mama? May I please be excused?"

The Hallelujah Chorus burst through the heavens, and I'm certain that confetti exploded from the ceiling.

There's no shame in repentance, only wisdom ...which only fools will shun.

Oh, friends...do you need to be excused? What should you do? *Do not be ashamed of the returning...*

Pardon and release, forgiveness and freedom come in the asking. Healing comes in the closeness. And then we can play, and rest.

Another day, another kid, also talking about some unfinished business. The sable kitten sat between us, moderating the discussion and softening the edges.

"Why can't I have *xyz* yet?" he asked, in so many words.

"Because you still have this situation from *efg* and *rst* that you haven't taken care of yet. And you need to apologize to your sister and brother for not minding your p's and q's, too."

What I meant was, *Dude, because you got busted and haven't cleaned up your mess yet.*

I really want him to have *xyz*. I want him to have the whole crazy alphabet. It's not my intention at all to lay a heavy burden on him, and I don't want him to feel defeated at every turn. But he's been making things hard on himself by piling up outstanding relational debt.

"I'm sorry. I'm sorry for *efg*."

"Thanks...I forgive you," I said, and waited to see if he would take responsibility for the rest.

But the long pause turned into a full stop. Nothing else. The business remained unfinished.

Undealt with, these situations are like pieces of grit building up in a pipe. If they're not irrigated quickly, they cement themselves in like so many embedded rocks. Eventually the choice to let things calcify becomes a habit, and what is meant to be a conduit is blocked entirely. A full stop. The Spirit can't flow through when we refuse to deal with the muck.

> *You were running well. Who hindered you*
> *from obeying the truth?*
>
> *– Galatians 5:7*

Resentment, bitterness, unforgiveness, and refusal to accept responsibility are grave hindrances to our effectiveness in prayer. They are rocks we trip over, boulders we butt up against, and we wonder why our prayers seem to go nowhere. Sometimes it's because we've let things pile up, and they've cemented right in the middle of the path we're walking.

But they don't have to stay there.

> *Therefore, confess your sins to one another*
> *and pray for one another, that you may be*
> *healed. The prayer of a righteous person*
> *has great power as it is working.*
>
> *– James 5:16*

Humility and repentance are the gentle dynamite that clears our path. It's not that He doesn't hear us, or doesn't want *xyz* and the rest of the whole crazy alphabet for us. Sometimes, we've got some unfinished business to attend to first.

It's not just my kids; I do this too. They might get their stubbornness from me (but don't tell Vince I said that). I vividly remember one night when I was supposed to be writing, and I needed to be on task, on a mission, meeting a deadline, and in bed before 3 am.

Instead, I was having a fit over a misdirected link on my website that took readers to a page that didn't exist. 404. Error. Sorry, no such page.

A calm, cool-headed, normal person would've shrugged and dealt with it another time. Tomorrow maybe, or next week. But, no. *Ohh*, no – that bad boy was going to get fixed come hell or high water, and it was going to get fixed now. Immediately – just as soon as I could figure out html, 404 re-directs, meta-data code, and other technical things I know next to nothing about. Posthaste. Chop-chop.

Truth is, I'm not even sure how to change the ink in our wireless printer. I avoid going into the website's backstage bleep-bloop room to fix techy stuff at all costs, afraid I'll break something. So I searched for every other option possible on Earth, under the Earth, in Middle Earth, it didn't matter. Anything but the bleep-bloop room.

An hour later, more confused than ever and the clock ticking, I broke down and went to that back office of our server, with virtual wires buzzing and lights flashing and files of mysterious technical icons and doohickies.

I've been in this situation many times before, trying to avoid something essential out of fear, uncertainty, or stubbornness, only to come up against that critical issue again and again, until I finally give in and deal with it.

I poked around for a while. Open file, close file. Open different file, close file. Back to the home page. *Oh, looky there...an icon labeled "redirects." Whaddaya know.*

Once I was in the right place, it took ninety seconds to fix. *Shannon Guerra, hacking ninja.*

There have been prayers I've avoided because they were about issues I didn't want to deal with. I thought that once I mentioned it to God, it would be this giant can of worms and I'd be up all night hashing things out and crying ugly tears and going to therapy for the next six months.

But no. Oh, no. I mean, sometimes those things are necessary, but not usually. He's much more efficient than that.

Once I gave in, at the speed of thought He was right there to bring truth, wisdom, conviction, healing. In a flash, a transaction of forgiveness occurred – from Him to me, from me to others. It happens swiftly when we let Him. Posthaste. Immediately.

We've been trying to teach our kids this as we learn it ourselves: He speaks in the surrender.

He is gentle and forgiving where we are stubborn and hard, and He helps us to be brave, transparent, unafraid to face responsibility, and move on.

We let go of what hinders and the rubble slides away. The Spirit flows through again, and effective prayer runs in torrents.

Now the Lord is the Spirit, and where the Spirit of the Lord is, there is freedom.

– 2 Corinthians 3:17

I had something all written up and ready to publish before deadline, and then felt a firm nudge to switch gears entirely. I prayed, *Oh, no...You want me to write about that? I have two days left. You're kidding, right?*

He answered, *Nope, Love, not kidding. Guess you'd better get to work, hmm?*

For days I had sat down with a project and couldn't get the green light no matter how many hours I stared at the keyboard and willed it to come together. Something else was percolating underneath and I needed to stop resisting so He could pour it out.

So I started over. *Tabula rasa*, adios, erased. But don't worry, I saved it elsewhere to use some other time; writers squirrel this stuff away like quilters hoard fabric.

And then I told Vince, "I need to get this done by Monday night, no ifs, ands, or buts."

The impudent man replied, "Well, I'm going to be watching football that night. Which sports bar would you like me to take the kids to?"

He was kidding, of course. I actually spent some time in bars as a kid – not sneaking in as a teen with fake ID, but swinging my short legs off the barstool in the afternoon, sitting with inebriates and locals, because my dad worked there. I didn't know then that it wasn't the place for a little girl to be, even in the '80s – but looking back, I remember Dad telling me that Grandma had some strong opinions about it, and though he was a young single dad, he was man enough to admit she was probably right.

Probably none of us had sterile childhoods. But while I saw many drunk adults as I was growing up (most of them weren't in bars), my dad was never one of them. He was my biggest fan at every school event he could make the hour's drive to. He took me on my first hike, helped me catch my first fish, and taught me to love country music.

But I'm not who I was back then. Blonde pigtails and a bad temper, crass and uncouth, with no boundaries and all sorts of fears and insecurities. I didn't know it wasn't the way a girl should be. It's been a long road to self-respect and learning how to reflect a Father who loves without any imperfection.

> *And you were dead in the trespasses and sins in which you **once walked** [used to, but not anymore], following the course of this world, following the prince of the power of the air, the spirit that is now at work in the sons of disobedience — among whom **we all once lived** in the passions of our flesh [past tense], carrying out the desires of the body and the mind, and **were** [not "are] by nature children of wrath, like the rest of mankind.*

> *But God—*

I love this part. Ready?

> **But God,** *being rich in mercy, because of the great love with which he loved us, even when we were dead in our trespasses,* **made us alive** *together with Christ — by grace* **you have been saved** — *and* **raised us up with him** *and* **seated us with him in the heavenly places** *in Christ Jesus.*
>
> *- Ephesians 2:1-6, with a few of my interruptions*

I'm still a work in progress. Metamorphosis is painful, and probably the most significant way I can tell He's maturing me is that now I let Him work in spite of the pain.

> *It might be good if we stopped using the terms "victory" and "defeat" to describe our progress of holiness. Rather we should use the terms "obedience" and "disobedience."*
>
> *- Jerry Bridges* [3]

The enemy doesn't care what side of the horse we fall off of — whether we lie and justify our sins to ourselves, or whether we go to the other extreme, pretending to be responsible for all the sins of others and feeling sorry for ourselves under the weight of it all. He just doesn't want us to stay in the saddle.

Family transitions and major life changes have a way of refining us, bubbling impurities to the surface that we'd rather not have to deal with. We feel the struggle, strain, and pain on the upward climb, not the downhill slope. We are breathless from the effort that achieves progress, not the easy plateau.

One afternoon, our big kids were working on assignments and the little kids were playing. Our school time isn't complex; the rule here is that assignments need to be finished before playtime, and those who are already playing need to do so quietly while others are still working.

And Afton was done, so he went upstairs to play. So far, so good.

But suddenly, as loud as it could go, the *Star Wars* soundtrack erupted from his stereo.

Two of the kids were still in the middle of math and I was under a lapful of papers and a sleeping kitten, so I hollered over the noise for him to turn the music off. Reagan sat on the floor among her Legos with her arm over her face, rocking, which she does when she's overstimulated, scared, or startled. The combination of Afton's music and my shouting did the trick.

The music went off. There was silence for a few seconds. And then Afton came downstairs crying, thinking he was in trouble. He had wanted to do something funny and instead of succeeding, he was yelled at. He annoyed his brother who was trying to do long division in algebra, he scared his sister, and his mom yelled at him, and he was beyond deflated. He said he never wanted to do his fun idea again. Never, ever.

He couldn't tell me why, though. He didn't know the name for what he was feeling. I knew what it was, though, because I've felt it many times myself. Shame.

It comes in a few different shades of darkness, but in Afton's case, the enemy took something that needed a small correction and blew it out of proportion in his heart. He wants to convince us that we are bad, instead of the sin or the mistake. That big liar.

Afton and I sat on the couch working through some hard, deep thoughts for an eight-year-old. He was wearing his favorite shorts, which, though already stained to high heaven, were also coated with a fresh layer of dirt from playing outside earlier.

I asked him if we should throw his shorts away or just wash them at bedtime. He scrunched his eyebrows at me in an are-you-crazy kind of look and said, "They're my favorites."

"Well, they're really dirty. Do you want to wear them again?" I asked.

"They're my favorite shorts. Let's just wash them."

"Huh...do you think you could do the same thing with your idea? Instead of throwing it away, can we just, you know, wash it? Then try it again?"

Sniffle. "Maybe."

The enemy convinces us the entire thing was wrong, everything associated with our experience was humiliating. But in reality, it's just dirt that needs washing.

We don't always need to burn every bridge associated with whatever it was, though sometimes it might be a good idea. But when we do something bad, we don't throw ourselves away. We throw away the shame, and wash in Him. It's how He saved us.

They only were hearing it said, "He who used to persecute us is now preaching the faith he once tried to destroy." And they glorified God because of me.

- Galatians 1:23-24

Refinement, major transitions, and new normals are hard. If you're like me when you're in a season of painful change, the phrase "new normal" might even tick you off because you don't want the upheaval to be normal at all – you want the old normal back. The old normal was comfortable, safe, even sacred compared to this new mess we find ourselves in.

I'm learning that if He's called you to it, the new normal will get there, too. On the other side it does eventually start to feel comfortable, and even safe (ish). It will certainly feel sacred; it's something you fought for. The old normal won't be diminished, but you will be expanded, like visiting a childhood haunt that seems so much smaller. It's not because it shrank; it's because you grew up.

But for now, you're in the middle of growing pains and it's excruciating. It's not a scenic bridge to cross – it's all the awkwardness and agony of middle school, for crying out loud. The transition is hard but temporary. Listen to me...*it is temporary.*

I say this to you as a friend who has been to the scenic bridge, fallen off after the first few steps, and clawed her way up the cliff on the other side. And I won't sugarcoat it, it took a few years. When I look back at the trail of blood, sweat, and tears, I'm grateful for where we are now.

Every year, we're not who we used to be. By His grace we're more like who we're meant to be.

God cares about you and your situation – your past, and your future. And any mess that you are in right now? He has good plans for it. Not a thing is wasted.

You are the best, you-est you as you move further into the future He has for you. Still you, but refined. Golden. Blooming, with new wings.

> *From now on, therefore, we regard no one according to the flesh. Even though we once regarded Christ according to the flesh, we regard him thus no longer. Therefore, if anyone is in Christ, he is a new creation. The old has passed away; behold, the new has come. All this is from God, who through Christ reconciled us to himself and gave us the ministry of reconciliation.*
>
> *– 2 Corinthians 5:16-18*

Most of us can run from our past, but it takes strength to face it, sift through the rubble, and let God wash through it.

The enemy wants us to be cowards: weak, and easily manipulated. Any wretch can deny, lie, or persist in wrong thinking or wrong behavior. It takes guts to turn your face toward light when you've been hiding in shadows.

It takes a special kind of bravery to admit fault, be teachable, and turn. It takes grit and valor to start over.

> *I thank him who has given me strength, Christ Jesus our Lord, because he judged me faithful, appointing me to his service,*

*though formerly I was a blasphemer,
persecutor, and insolent opponent. But I
received mercy because I had acted ignor-
antly in unbelief, and the grace of our Lord
overflowed for me with the faith and love
that are in Christ Jesus.*

- 1 Timothy 1:12-14

Tabula rasa. It's okay – sometimes it's even
best – to start over. He won't waste a thing.

*The saying is trustworthy and deserving of
full acceptance, that Christ Jesus came into
the world to save sinners, of whom I am
the foremost. But I received mercy for this
reason, that in me, as the foremost, Jesus
Christ might display his perfect patience as
an example to those who were to believe in
him for eternal life. To the King of the ages,
immortal, invisible, the only God, be honor
and glory forever and ever. Amen.*

- 1 Timothy 1:15-17

God made a way for shame to leave, for you to
live free. Shame off you, shame off me. We are the
washed ones – covered by Him, and at the same
time, set free.

We were running a little late to church the
following Sunday morning. One of the kids was
sick, and we made a last-minute decision for everyone to stay home except for Mattie and I since we
were both scheduled to serve. We peeled into the
parking lot just in time, and I don't know what the
song is called or who was singing it, but the last
thing we heard on the country station before

shutting off the ignition was something about a lady standing on her front porch with a shotgun.

Bless her heart. It could've been me.

Some of you probably know the name of the song...I like you rascals.

She frowns almost every time I see her. Snappish, and sad. And usually by herself.

No, not my reflection in the mirror. Someone else, I hardly know her. I saw her again recently and smiled, tried to talk to her, but I got a little slimed. Rebuffed.

I thought, "Why is she so grumpy?" but that wasn't the real question at the root of my feelings.

The forefront of my mind was thinking, "Retreat!" but in the back of my mind, I was really asking, "Why doesn't she like me?"

I asked Him, Did I do something?

No. She acts that way because she's wounded. She doesn't like herself, and she's forgotten how much I like her. It has nothing to do with you...

Oh, good. Phew.

...but you do the same thing to your kids when you're grumpy.

Yikes. Ouch.

You don't get grumpy just because you're tired or frustrated; it's that you don't like yourself in that moment, and you've forgotten how much I like you, too.

I know you don't want to give your kids that message, He says. *Stay in close. Pray without ceas-*

ing for yourself and for others to know Me well. So much is at stake in this one thing.

> *I do not cease to give thanks for you, remembering you in my prayers, that the God of our Lord Jesus Christ, the Father of glory, may give you the Spirit of wisdom and of revelation in the knowledge of Him, having the eyes of your hearts enlightened, that you may know what is the hope to which He has called you...*
>
> *- Ephesians 1:16-18*

Rudeness only looks like dislike of others, He told me, *though it usually has nothing to do with their feelings about someone else. It has to do with their vision of themselves. And manners, too...but mostly it's how they see themselves, and how they see Me.*

He tells us, *You have more than you can imagine. When you look in the mirror, sometimes you hardly know that person. You have no idea who you're dealing with.*

He really wanted me to understand this. One day I woke up with curly hair, after almost forty years of hair so straight it couldn't be persuaded by a curling iron's highest setting.

For about eighteen months I had let it grow out and it was suddenly super frizzy. When stray hairs escaped from being pulled back, they looked suspiciously like ringlets...and I've never had ringlets. So, assuming that a good cut would tame the jungle, I made an appointment and got my standard biennial bob between chin and shoulder.

I drove home with dramatic 1930's waves, but thought they were just the magical results of the stylist's skill with a brush and hairdryer. It felt downright va-va-voomish. But I showered that night, washed like normal, and woke up the next morning with wild, misbehaving curls that went far beyond Va Va Voom and well into Holy Mackerel.

There was no magical stylist. It was choppy hormones working under the radar, and once my hair was several inches shorter it lost all inhibitions. It took some getting used to, and eventually calmed to mostly waves; sometimes I even go out in public without straightening it.

As a kid I actually wanted curly hair, and got a perm instead — a foolish thing no middle schooler should ever be forced to endure, no matter how much she begs for it — and it didn't take at all. I had long blond hair (sigh, those were the days), but none of the spirals that $75 promised to deliver in the late eighties. Just drippy, slack kinks.

It wasn't the right time yet. Like a thoughtful parent (because He is one), I think He tucked that idea away and waited to surprise me with it.

He keeps reminding me about putting on a new self, more of Him. Less control, more letting go, and letting Him express Himself through me.

You have no idea who you're dealing with, He told me. Not threatening, but gently patient. *Who you're dealing with is Myself, and yourself, in ways you've never known or seen before.*

About Himself, He said, *I love you more than you can imagine. I am bigger than you can imagine. You have no idea Who you're dealing with. I want to show you, so you can show others.*

It's the time of fruition, of fullness, He said. *This is the time for reaching upwards and outwards, boldly expressing My truth and love in a way that is wilder than you have ever done before. It is the right time now. It may be untamed, but I want to be set loose in your life without encumbrance or inhibition.*

He's given you a way to express His love and truth in a way that might surprise you. It has nothing to do with curly hair, but everything to do with getting rid of the weight of our past and reminding us of desires and dreams we have for the future.

We thought they were just passing fancies or crazy daydreams.

But He's saying, *No. I'm serious.*

For this is the will of God, that by doing good you should put to silence the ignorance of foolish people. Live as people who are free, not using your freedom as a cover up for evil, but living as servants of God.

- 1 Peter 2:15-16

One morning I was in the bathroom getting ready for the day – probably trying to figure out what to do with my hair, since I've never mastered curls – and our four-year-old was with me.

Upon discovering that she could reach the bathroom faucet, she burst out, "I grew! God stretched me when I was sleeping last night!" She paused. "Only He did it very gently, not like when people do it."

It seemed like it happened overnight, though it had been in the works, in His plan and timing, for days, weeks, months, until she noticed she could do it. It wasn't forced, it wasn't rushed, and it wasn't contrived.

It was the perfect time for her to reach new heights.

And it might be for us, too.

threshold:

THE LINK BETWEEN DREAMS AND OBEDIENCE

For, "Yet a little while, and the coming one will come and will not delay; but my righteous one shall live by faith, and if he shrinks back, my soul has no pleasure in him."

But we are not of those who shrink back and are destroyed, but of those who have faith and preserve their souls.

Hebrews 10:37-39

Moonbeams slant across the floor. I'm up again in the middle of the night, probably from too much water at bedtime and not enough water during the day.

Jesus, we've got to stop meeting this way. I smile, sort of.

A trip to the bathroom and back to bed, and the striped cat who followed me makes himself comfortable on my feet (who needs hot water bottles?) while the white cat – these two are just like salt and pepper, really – curls up within arm's reach. Vince slept through all of our jostling and the house is quiet.

I'm awake though, and I know the drill. But instead of praying I backslide into the opposite.

A list of concerns starts parading through my thoughts: Bad habits cropping up in some of our children. Sneaky behavior cropping up in others. Appointments I keep forgetting to make. A rash on Chamberlain's face, an allergy that I can't figure out, especially at three in the morning...and I'm seriously fretting, overwhelmed, and feeding the beast.

I'm tired, and in the middle of the night my to-do list looks so magnified that I feel done in before the day has even had a chance to start.

Hey, Love, He says. *Your night vision is inflating your problems.*

Try a different point of view: Magnify Me instead. Picture the victory.

It's hard at first. I try to imagine a child – one who lies in both words and actions – being honest in his words and actions, and attached to us. It feels so far off that it takes me a while to even think of what that would look like. But I get it after a few minutes, and then in less than two seconds it becomes prayer.

It's the breakthrough we're praying toward.

Over and over, with every issue He reminds me: *Picture the victory.*

My list is long, but He's not tired and I'm not going anywhere. He's right there, ready to tackle the big stuff with me.

I picture a normal, routine day, minus the ever-present walking on eggshells and constant high alert status.

I picture snuggles given freely, assignments done quickly. I picture health issues, gone.

This isn't some new-age piffle. It's scripture, obeyed:

> *...in the presence of the God in whom he believed, who gives life to the dead and calls into existence the things that do not exist.*
>
> - *Romans 4:17b*

> *Therefore I tell you, whatever you ask in prayer, believe that you have received it, and it will be yours.*
>
> - *Mark 11:24*

> *And Jesus answered them, "Truly, I say to you, if you have faith and do not doubt, you will not only do what has been done to the fig tree, but even if you say to this*

mountain, 'Be taken up and thrown into
the sea,' it will happen. And whatever you
ask in prayer, you will receive, if you have
faith."

- Matthew 21:21-22

I picture the victory of special needs healed,
casting mountains to the sea, because He can.
Because He wants to teach me how, and He wants
me to remember to do it instead of feeding anxiety
and letting it wreak havoc.

The day ahead becomes do-able. Fretting and
fears diminished. Faith and hope rising.

It's more than just my feelings – the future has
changed. We are the clean-up operation, working
the night shift.

The next night the moon is almost full, but
obscured by thin clouds and crisscrossed with the
silhouettes of branches in the woods. I'm not sure if
it's waxing or waning; I'm sorry to say I don't
usually pay attention to the stages of the moon.

I do pay very close attention to the status of
other things, though. Really important things.
Friends, I'm talking about life-altering things that
can affect the direction of our entire day. Like the
phases of coffee.

Behold, a sampling: Empty. Full. Half-full.
Half-caff. Partly cloudy. No sugar, just cream.
Stirred, not shaken. And never, ever, spilled on the

computer, thank you very much – been there, done that, got the new laptop to show for it.

And then, there's decaf. Poor decaf. We call it names, push it to the back of the cabinet, and make jokes about it (You heard the one about how coffee is made? Real coffee is made from the beans from the coffee plant, but decaf is made from dirt the plant is growing in) but for all that, I admit there is a time and a place for decaf. For example, late at night, by a warm fire, when I don't want to be up with the tremors until 5 am – that is a great time for decaf.

No matter what the phase of my coffee, my thoughts wander all over the place as I go through the minutes of the day. Here's a 20-second glimpse while getting a glass of water:

Wow, this kitchen is a disaster. I can't even see the counter. The dishes will have to wait till tomorrow, I still have to get tonight's post done. But it's a huge mess – which of the kids is going to clean that up tomorrow? I should clean it up now. It's gross. And the shower door still needs cleaned. I need to do that, too – no, I'll assign that to a different kid. I'll just clean up the veggie peels – hey, who put the butter knife in the compost bin? I wonder if that's where all of our plastic spoons have gone. Wait, where did I put my water glass?

These are Decaf Thoughts. They're drowsy, heavy-yoked, and splashing all over the place. Not particularly productive, not creating momentum.

The big and little events of the day can shake us or they can stir us. We can respond with dull lethargy or be stirred to unceasing prayer that is productive, creative, and fruitful, instead of just reacting to life around us.

I try it again:

Jesus, thanks for the amazing dinner. Thanks for the dishes, and the kitchen. I love having a dishwasher, and all my little dishwashing helpers. I really, really love plumbing and hot showers. I need Your words for a good post tonight to encourage the readers You send. I have no idea what to write about yet, but I'm trusting that You have it all prepared for me. Please remind the kids not to throw away their silverware. And if You'd help them to stop breaking dishes, that would be awesome, too.

Just a change in perspective, from focusing on the mess to partnering with the One who has answers and wisdom for it. We go from clumsy shaking to light-yoked stirring, regardless of the phase of our coffee.

In this season, out of six kids we have two fluent readers, one still learning to read, and three who are just grasping letters and sounds. We have letters everywhere, books everywhere, pencils and crayons and paper all over the place, floor to ceiling.

A year ago Afton was just starting to sound out words, and now he is devouring *Frog and Toad*, *Mr. Putter and Tabby*, and *Fox in Socks*. He loves gardening, cooking, food – he's just like a hobbit really, minus the pipeweed and ale – and soon he'll be able to read about all of these things to himself. A huge world will open to him.

Dr. Seuss is just the floor. There's so much more.

It's a lot of work, though. Often, he'd rather we just read things for him than do it himself. I can't blame him too much. I have hard things I'd rather not try to sound out, also – those painful situations I really don't even want to touch because it raises ugliness up.

I'm still working on picturing the victory. He said, *Don't think of where it is right now – that's the floor. Think of the ceiling.*

Pray from joy, from victory to victory. From floor to ceiling, and then the next level up. There's always more.

I can do this for a million things. My efforts as a mother, a friend, a writer, a wife; healing for our kids, our hearts, our loved ones. Joy...I can picture joy. Most days I even hold it right here, with both hands. The light is getting brighter.

I don't want to be stuck at Dr. Seuss forever. I want Jane Austen, I want Charles Dickens, I want to finish the 1200-page copy of *Les Miserables* that's taking me forever to push through – I even want Plutarch, Socrates, and other old, dead Greek and Roman guys. Someday.

So I start telling Him all about it: Where we've come from, where we're at, where we're going, and where I want to be.

He says, *That's a great start.*

That's only My floor, though. There's so much more.

Oh. And, whoa.

He might be saying it to you, too.

One Saturday night after the kids and books are all tucked in, I'm praying in the shower and getting ready for bed, thinking of what our ceiling might look like. Plotting, planning, dreaming, shampooing – and I've read about how important it is to write these things down, so I'm excited to talk to Vince about it with a pen and paper. I rinse, grab a towel, and leave a trail of wet footprints in my enthusiasm to find a notebook and tell Vince all about it.

But the light was off and he was already asleep. My shower was long, and his day was too. His Saturdays start much earlier than mine.

It's okay, God said. *Save it for tomorrow. Sabbaths are good for dreaming.*

For a second, I worry that I'll forget it all by tomorrow. Sometimes I think of wonderfully brilliant things and then immediately forget them, just to remember the faintest inkling of...what was it...fading like mist, recalling just enough to be annoyed with myself for forgetting the rest of it.

But He immediately reminded me of this incredible verse. He said it to the disciples after He gave them a whole slew of information to process, and they probably never had notebooks handy, either.

> *But the Helper, the Holy Spirit, whom the Father will send in my name, he will teach you all things **and bring to your remembrance all that I have said to you**.*
>
> *- John 14:26*

He said, *I'll be there to remind you about the ceiling tomorrow. I won't forget. I've never for-*

gotten what I have planned for you – and I'll help
you sound out all of the hard spots, too.

As we continue to pray relentless-style – right
as we're doing the dishes, changing diapers, driving
to work, encouraging a friend, and telling the phone
solicitor for the umpteenth time, *No, I don't have*
ten minutes to answer just a few questions – we
are storming castles. Right then, as we are praying,
abiding, recognizing His presence in every moment,
the captives are being set free.

But this doesn't mean that praying without
ceasing is a "stay in your comfort zone free" card.
Praying does not let us off the hook in serving
others, getting involved, giving extravagantly, or
anything else that gets our hands dirty. Our mission
is firmly outside the comfort zone.

What unceasing prayer will do is give us
greater wisdom for how He wants us to accomplish
those things, which eliminates much of the anxiety
and discomfort that doing them might cause otherwise. And this is important, because He will ask us
to do things that feel bigger than we are.

Sometimes He asks us to do something that
seems like it's not "you." What if His prompting
feels too intimidating, too unfamiliar, too hard, too
new?

It can be a big or a little thing. It might be
something like tackling a classic for the first time –
and don't tell anyone, but when I first read *Sense*
and Sensibility, I was so confused I couldn't tell the

difference between Fanny and Elinor Dashwood. But later I approached *Anna Karenina* with fear and trembling and discovered that those tricky Russian authors have three different names for each character, which really messed me up. I went back to British literature with a better attitude after that.

Or, it might be that He's talking to us about a Big Thing. That thing we can't stop thinking about but feels out of reach, or that Next Big Thing that we keep pushing to the back of our minds because we have no idea how to begin it. And we're nervous about talking to someone about it or even praying about it because, well, when you do that, things might get a little more serious... and we're not so sure we want it to be serious.

And He tells us, *Oh, Love...who do you think you are, anyway?*

Don't you really want to know who you are? Because you're so much more than who you limit yourself to be inside the safety of your comfort zone.

This habit of relentless prayer broadens the limits that we set for ourselves. Little steps become big steps. Those big steps get easier and start to feel like little steps. And before you know it, your comfort zone has grown deep and wide and you're still pushing the edges of it outward.

You, pursuing that thing He's called you to. Me, pursuing that thing He called me to. Fearless, relentless, while we pray for our country and its messes, and our families and their future, and the active clean-up operation in our own hearts, and suddenly, that castle is ours.

Sunday evening. Throughout the day, Vince and I checked in with each other about putting things on paper, and it was finally time. Dreaming is for every day, but especially the Sabbath, when rest draws us near to the Dream-maker.

The kids were tucked in, it was quiet, and we had a notebook and a pen. We started our list, bouncing ideas back and forth.

"In no particular order, right?" I asked. Vin nodded.

And God said, *In no particular order...write. Just write. Call it your Christmas List.* So we did.

Vince and Shannon's Christmas List was fourteen items long of some pretty audacious schemes and dreams, and it made any residual legalism in me quiver a little to write them.

Times are hard in some places. The enemy threatens without and within, which is all the more reason to retaliate with a bigger vision. Ignore the hiss of the snake and start writing anyway.

Ugliness is out there, work needs to be done, and healing needs to come. It's because of this that we so badly need to listen. He dreams over us. We get to partner with Him in making the days ahead better simply by believing Him and then acting like it.

We write everything down, and it goes from some airy, tenuous vision to something defined, wrapped up in words. And we look at it and think, "Now what?"

He says, *Watch Me.*

A light shines in, because a door opens when we put words on paper. A breeze wafts past us, and the air that blows through smells different.

He has questions for me, for us.

If it didn't matter what anyone else thought...

If it didn't matter who noticed...

If it didn't matter who paid attention...

What would you let Me do in your life?

I had no idea where He was going with this. I can think of smallish, simple things in my realm of capability, but the big picture? No idea.

How would you let Me move?

Where would you let Me take you?

I can write a list and come up with all kinds of crazy ideas, but for them to become more than just words on paper I have to give Him permission to move in me, through me, around me. And when I think of what that means, it's a little Be Careful What You Ask For-ish.

He asks us, *Can I carry you over the threshold?*

So many times this year, I thought I met my threshold for change, growth, and painful stretching.

It's a different kind of threshold, He says. *The kind that is a doorway. It means Beginning, Birth, Dawn, Entrance.*

Do I really want what's on this list? I tend to backpedal, thinking of what it means.

It means change. Not sudden, probably, but change for sure. And the frustrating thing about change is that it's always so...different. Sheesh. We've had enough of that for a while, haven't we?

Not like this, He says. *Will you let Me?* An open doorway means nothing if we don't walk through it.

But what if we don't know which way to go? What if our threshold is more like a fork in the road?

God...just tell me. Which way? Do I focus on this thing, or that thing? We ask for doors to open, doors to shut, and when we go to check, they're swinging back and forth on their hinges. This isn't what I asked for.

He says, *What did you ask for, Love?*

And I think, oh...nothing much. Just an answer – a clear answer. A neon sign. Something really bright with flashing arrows would be just about perfect.

I don't usually use those. Especially when I already told you what to do. And there's the rub.

> *He said, "But I will be with you, and **this shall be the sign for you**, that I have sent you: **when you have brought the people out of Egypt,** [obeyed in doing what I already told you to do] you shall serve God on this mountain."*
>
> *– Exodus 3:12*

> *And **when the soles of the feet** of the priests bearing the ark of the Lord, the Lord of all the earth, **shall rest in the waters** of the Jordan, **the waters of the Jordan shall be cut off from flowing,** and the waters coming down from above shall stand in one heap."*
>
> *– Joshua 3:13*

Step in. You have to get your feet wet first. Walk where I tell you, and then watch Me hold the waters back.

Sometimes confirmation comes after obedience, not before. God is not a micromanager. If His instructions are clear but we're still asking for confirmation, our problem is probably not in knowing His will – it's in following through and doing His will. The waters won't move for us while we stall at the shoreline.

We think we want a sign for directions, but the sign He wants to give us is recognition for achievement – a crown. We can be so busy asking for excuses not to use our faith that we miss the opportunity to win the prize at the end of obedience.

Sometimes when we say we are waiting on Him, the truth is we're just not trusting Him. We settle for so little in the stalling to obey.

How do we tell the difference? Are we stalling, or are we waiting?

Did you do what I already told you, Love?

Well, yes. I mean, sort of. Mostly, I think.

I sound a lot like my sons when I ask them if they made their beds in the morning. Almost always, the truth is...no. *No, not really. I didn't really do it all the way, just sorta spread the top blanket around to cover up the wrinkly sheets underneath. I thought that would be good enough.*

God tells me the same thing I tell them: *Go back and check again. Dig a little deeper, more than just making things look good on the surface. Do it right once, and you won't have to do it over and over. You won't have to keep asking me if it's done, because you'll know it is.*

When we are stalling, looking for a sign, what we're really asking is, *Is it good enough?*

How do we know if we're stalling, or waiting? When we are truly waiting on Him, we're all-in and have obeyed in taking that step outside the comfort zone. We won't be looking for a back-up plan, because we didn't bring one.

We need not, when abed, to lie awake to talk with God; He can visit us while we sleep, and cause us then to hear His voice. Our heart oft-times wakes when we sleep, and God can speak to that, either by works, by proverbs, by signs and similitudes, as well as if one was awake.

— John Bunyan [1]

Winter finally came and the trees hung heavy with snow. It felt bookish, like the evenings were made for tea and thought and rest, but there was so much to do my brain was dizzy thinking of it. Dishes always need washing and children always need bathing, and laundry always needs, well, laundering.

But instead of doing any of that, I sat under a blanket, under a cat, and under a few deadlines. Eating ice cream for dinner and studying was the most productive way to procrastinate that I could think of without having to leave the couch.

I'd been working through Brother Lawrence's *The Practice of the Presence of God* — just a tiny thing, my copy is about 100 pages, but it goes in small chunks that fill you immediately. Like lembas bread, for us nerdy, literary types.

While sharing bites of ice cream with the cat, I read this:

> God...has infinite treasure to bestow, and we take up with a little sensible devotion which passes in a moment. Blind as we are, we hinder God and stop the current of His graces. [2]

I have to read it a couple of times to take it all in. Sophie swipes at the spoon hanging in midair while I mull it over, wondering if I've hindered His current lately by settling for less than He wanted to give. So much is at stake in His flowing through us.

> But when He finds a soul penetrated with a lively faith, He pours into it His graces and favors plentifully; there they flow like a torrent, which, after being forcibly stopped against its ordinary course, when it has found a passage, spreads itself with impetuosity and abundance. [3]

A soul penetrated with lively faith is a trust in Him that stirs up the waters. The peace in our spirit is directly proportional to the wild activity of our faith. And we have no lack of wild activity around here; what we need is to channel it to the right current so it actually produces something other than unrest.

> ...Not to advance in the spiritual life is to go back. But those who have the gale of the Holy Spirit go forward even in sleep. If the

vessel of our soul is still tossed with winds and storms, let us awake the Lord, who reposes in it, and He will quickly calm the sea. 4

He's been trying to tell me something: *The more audacious your faith is, the more settled your spirit will be.* There goes that comfort zone again. Bye-bye, ciao, adios...

As our faith becomes more radical, our spirit grows more resolved, rested, peaceful. We believe Him wildly and are moved with speed by the current of His grace, while our spirit is becalmed even in the midst of storm. Our spirit only finds rest when our faith is on the move.

This new season isn't about me. It's not about what I can do; it's about what He does. *Not to advance in the spiritual life is to go back...But those who have the gale of the Holy Spirit go forward even in sleep.* Deadlines are met. Children are bathed, books are read. And things actually get done. Maybe even the dishes.

You must believe that God is separate from the world and that some of the things we see in it are contrary to His will. Confronted with a cancer or a slum the Pantheist can say, "If you could only see it from the divine point of view, you realize that this also is God." The Christian replies, "Don't talk damned nonsense." For Christianity is a fighting religion. It thinks God made the

world.... But it also thinks that a great many things have gone wrong with the world that God made and that God insists, and insists very loudly, on our putting them right again.

– C.S. Lewis [5]

One kid is napping and five kids are out with Vince on a quick errand to get coffee and a new toilet seat (lest you were under the impression that life here is glamorous). He's getting coffee because something went horribly wrong with our coffee maker this morning, leaving the coffee ruined and putrid. And I guess you could say the same thing about the toilet seat, but I digress.

I started reading Joshua, which excites me because Jericho is coming and it's one of my favorites. But I'm not at Jericho yet. I'm at this part:

At that time the Lord said to Joshua, "Make flint knives and circumcise the sons of Israel a second time."

– Joshua 5:2

Oh.

And also, yuck. But necessary, I get it – this was the transitional generation, whose parents had shrunk back at the opportunity to take the Promised Land. This was their time take hold of it, but first they had to deal with this. It wasn't glamorous. It was the clean-up operation before the clean-up operation.

So it was their children, whom he raised up in their place, that Joshua circumcised.

*For they were uncircumcised, because they
had not been circumcised on the way.*

*When the circumcising of **the whole nation** was finished, they remained in their
places in the camp until they were healed.*

– Joshua 5:7-8

The task was huge. Joshua might have looked
across at the nation in a daze, wondering where to
start – sort of like how we look across at the news
and the events around us. It's that deer-in-the-
headlights stupor, knowing the times are urgent,
the dangers are imminent, and the needs are many.

The issues are delicate and lives are at stake.
We plunge in with caution – quick to obey, but
careful to clean up our own hearts before all else.

I'll show you what to focus on first, He said.
It's right in front of you.

*When you realize that your own heart and
obedience are the first thing to deal with, you are
protected from being overwhelmed and stupefied.
Surrender gives you a calm simplicity to just do
the first thing, and then the next thing. Simple
steps, consistent prayer, steady progress.*

Dinner that night is nothing fancy, just pasta
and veggies, and Chamberlain loves to chop mushrooms for me. She's at one end of the cutting board
while I'm at the other end, chopping the last two
slices of bacon that were left over from breakfast. It
takes me a while to realize Cham is holding the
knife upside down and using the blunt edge to cut
with.

"Turn it over," I tell her.

She does, and finishes the mushrooms. We toss them in with the onions and garlic already sautéing, add the bacon, and throw the noodles in the pot of boiling water. She runs off to play and I grab my Bible to read while the rotini cooks.

This is the part of Joshua I've been waiting for – where God reminds us that all of His instructions that don't make sense still come to fruition and victory, that all of our impossibilities are nothing but walls to march around in prayer, expectation, and worship.

It sounds beautiful. It sounds dramatic. It sounds...well, easy. We know this story: They march, they shout, the walls come down. But, like all of our stories, there's more to it than that.

> *The people came up out of the Jordan on the tenth day of the first month, and they encamped at Gilgal on the east border of Jericho.*
>
> – Joshua 4:19

The tenth day, they crossed the Jordan.

> *While the people of Israel were encamped at Gilgal, they kept the Passover on the fourteenth day of the month in the evening on the plains of Jericho.*
>
> – Joshua 5:10

On the fourteenth day, they celebrated the Passover. In between, they were dealing with some (cough) personal business we already discussed.

> *And the day after the Passover, on that*

very day, they ate of the produce of the land, unleavened cakes and parched grain.

– Joshua 5:11

The fifteenth day, they ate the food the land produced. And then they were in for it.

*And **the manna ceased** the day after they ate of the produce of the land. And there was no longer manna for the people of Israel, but they ate of the fruit of the land of Canaan that year.*

– Joshua 5:12

The manna ceased. Stopped. All done, finis. There was no going back, no back-up plan – the water was rushing in the Jordan River behind them, and in front of them was a fortified city to conquer. In between, they were all in.

Maybe if the manna had kept coming, some of them might have thought to go back to the river, hoping that God would hold back the water again and let them return. But no, this was a sharp knife, cutting off any hesitation to obey – no manna meant they were invested, they were staying, and the only direction they were going was forward.

And my life needs this. A commitment I need to let go of, an unhealthy relationship that needs firm boundaries, that threshold I need to walk through: I've been using the blunt edge of a knife to whack at them every once in a while, but those things have been on the cutting board for a long time. Probably way too long, and we're not getting anywhere.

Turn it over, He tells me. And I squirm a little about it, but He's right there, saying, *Don't hesitate to obey, Love. You are invested, you are staying, the only direction you're going is forward.*

Snow flew all over the place outside, and papers flew all over the place inside.

Vince took two weeks off so I could work on a special project while he homeschooled the kids. I cloistered upstairs in the Thinkery – just a small table by a window, covered in books, papers, a laptop, and a full pot of chai tea containing about ten cups of caffeinated goodness.

This particular project was part of Vince and Shannon's Christmas List that we wrote in the fall, and completing it directly related to obeying Him with the sharp knife and stepping through the threshold. But I'd been putting it off for over a year, and God sat me down for a talk.

He told me He had something wonderful for me if I would just hold out my hands and accept it. The problem was I was already holding onto something else, and I didn't want to let go.

And He was patient with me – because He is like that – and He said, *Whenever you're ready for it, Love. But how long do you really want to wait for Me to bless you with this?*

I realized I was being an idiot and stopped dragging my feet. I let go, grabbed hold, and hung on.

I'd been reading this:

And without faith it is impossible to please him, for whoever would draw near to God must believe that he exists and that he rewards those who seek him.

- Hebrews 11:6

And this:

*By faith Abraham obeyed when he was called to go out to a place that he was to receive as an inheritance. And he went out, **not knowing where he was going.***

- Hebrews 11:8

And also, this:

*In an age when leaders pass from the scene rapidly and without much loss, Churchill remains astoundingly relevant and contemporary. One suspects it will remain so for generations. The reason is that Churchill was, stating it plainly, **a wise man;** not a wise man in the sense of the eastern mystic, but rather of a man **who has lived deeply, whose wisdom was born in study, tempered in conflict, tested in crisis, and honed in reflection.** It was a wisdom beyond his own age, a kind that transcended his times and has relevance for every age in which men grapple with mighty causes.*

- Stephen Mansfield [6]

I'm convinced that when we follow Him into the wild, He draws us closer to Himself in a way that is intimate, game changing, and contagious. We live deeply and we have more to give to a world that needs Him desperately.

We, too, are a transitional generation; our nations will pivot their direction largely due to our obedience or lack thereof. We must know where we are headed and how to prepare for it.

forward:

FIGHTING FEAR

AND OTHER MINIONS

I remember the story of the old man who said on his deathbed that he had had a lot of trouble in his life, most of which had never happened.

Winston Churchill

Throughout my adulthood I've heard women rave about one thing, claiming it changed their lives forever. Entire blogs are devoted to the subject, and Pinterest is perfectly slathered with information on how to tap into its life-enhancing benefits.

I'm speaking of – you may drumroll now, if you'd like – The Amazing, The Miraculous, The Inexplicably Marvelous Phenomenon known as...a crock pot.

And yet I've been in the dark all this time. Never used it, wasn't really interested, don't care for gadgets and extra appliances. But women everywhere raved, "Just throw your ingredients in, and dinner magically appears several hours later!" So, sometime after having six kids I decided that, maybe, I could use a little more magic in the culinary area of my life. Sold!

I chopped. I tossed in ingredients. I put the lid on. *This is going to be awesome,* I thought.

Except it wasn't. Two hours later, investigation revealed that it probably *does* work perfectly, unless you forget one thing: That plugging-it-in part is really, crucially, super important.

I don't really need magic, anyway. What I need is some quiet, focused attention so I can see what needs to be done and then just do it, without being overwhelmed with the other fourteen things I feel like I should also be doing in that very moment. Also, a housekeeper would be nice.

But I had this audacious list and we stood right at the doorway of opportunity, and I had to choose either to keep hesitating or move forward. We asked God for these Big Things and we were at the threshold of whatever this newness is, a little blinded by the light shining through, and not really sure what the other side looks like.

So I hesitate at the passage. There's a quavering in my gut, immediately followed by a zinging sound, and I duck. That was a close one.

> "Oh, the fool!" groaned the Hermit. "Poor, brave little fool. He knows nothing about this work. He's making no use at all of his shield. His whole side's exposed. He hasn't the faintest idea what to do with his sword."
>
> - C.S. Lewis [1]

Not everyone wants us to walk through the door. There's greatness beyond and an enemy who doesn't want us to go there. Arrows are flying – words from others, words in my head, situations that seem less than ideal and more than a little impossible at times – and I'm still putting salve on a few spots where they hit their mark over the last few years and had to be yanked out, raw and bleeding. Forward growth is messy.

But He's right there at the passage with me. *You don't have to duck, you know,* He says.

Really? I straighten up, a little sheepish. (Did anyone see that?)

You have what you need to walk through safely, He says. *You just have to remember how to operate it.*

The crockpot does nothing when it's turned off; neither does my faith when I waver.

In all circumstances take up the shield of faith, with which you can extinguish all the flaming darts of the evil one.

- Ephesians 6:16

I've given you a picture of the victory, Love. Hold it high.

That faith – that vision, picturing the victory He has ahead – is our shield. It covers and protects our families and our marriages. And it is really, crucially, super important.

Hold it high, He says. *And don't hesitate when I tell you to move.*

When we go through a passage or stand at a threshold, it's exciting, right? I mean, in an I-hope-I-don't-puke-in-front-of-anyone kind of way. Praise the Lord and pass the Pepto.

But it's a struggle. I get this sinking, dropping feeling right under my ribs, a volley of fiery arrows the enemy uses every time I'm at the threshold of anything. Sometimes I fight it for days in a row, first thing in the morning, right out of the gate.

It's called fear and it wants to be entertained. It's an attention seeker, a bully, an insecure narcissist with no vision of its own. Instead, it steals your vision, warps and counterfeits it, and hands it back to you posing as the real deal – only, by that time, it's ugly and twisted. Completely unrecognizable.

I have no intention of entertaining the beast or giving it any attention it doesn't deserve. We'll look at it just long enough to aim and fire and put it out of our misery.

This is personal. I hope you're okay with that.

For about six months a year, our birch trees are just naked trunks and bare sticks. In winter there's no green, no growing, no visible showing of anything happening under the surface for those of us here on the ground looking up at their exposed branches.

Over the last few years when the days are long, worries are loud, and it looks like there's no green growth happening anywhere, this niggling pain intrudes on me. It tries to mask itself by sounding like regret, but it's not regret. It's an accusation trying to get me to believe it.

Years ago we followed God into this radical thing called adoption – it was always His idea, not ours, because He can be such a troublemaker – and a conversation happened in the beginning of that process that still rears its ugly head in hard days. It happened before we brought Andrey and Reagan home, before our life had a bigger audience, before we became a part of multiple adoption communities and heard the accusations complete strangers sometimes level at adoptive families who are just trying to do the work God assigned them.

It was before all of that. It was personal.

It was this statement, said by someone who ought to know better, but in truth, knew very little:

"You won't be the mother you could be to your real kids once you bring those other kids into your home."

For real. Not kidding, not making it up, and not even bitter, believe it or not. If you could hear my tone through typed letters, it's just sad.

Hey, you birch tree. Your leaves are gone, and now you're nothing but a bunch of sticks. Look at you. It's over.

No, in all these things we are more than conquerors through him who loved us.

- *Romans 8:37*

But this wasn't my idea. It was His, and we followed Him across that threshold, up that bare tree, shedding leaves, privacy, familiarity, and the warmth of the comfort zone, and we are still following Him.

He told me, *Love, I'm going to give you more than you can handle because I want you to remember that you need Me. You can always trust Me.* But we heard from earthly, grounded voices that our heads were in the clouds.

We need (*neeeed*, listen to me say it in three syllables) His strength and protection, because He often tells us to do things that are absurd. Our obedience in departing the comfort zone offends some people; it makes them uncomfortable, like it might be catching. Contagious. And it is.

What terrifies others is becoming ho-hum to you because you've let Me move through you. Let Me surprise you with how much I am making you capable of.

Those who are on the front lines of a battle come under the heaviest fire, He reminds me often. *But I am your covering. I am above and below, before you and behind you, and in you to do strong, mighty things. I have your back.*

When I really needed it, He had me reading about other leaders who made hard choices.

*People who are not prepared to do unpop-
ular things and to defy clamor are not fit
to be Ministers in times of stress.*

- Winston Churchill

And,

*It is not open to the cool bystander...to set
himself up as an impartial judge of events
which would never have occurred had he
outstretched a helping hand in time.*

- Churchill

And, "Criticism is easy, achievement is difficult." Yep, also Churchill. The guy knew a thing or
two about both warfare and friendly fire.

I knew it was only the voice of the enemy using
someone as a mouthpiece for his lies and hatred. It
was the mouth of Sauron, a false prophet spreading
doubt and planting fear. Nothing more.

I still know it. I do.

And yet I hear it on days when I feel whipped,
when it feels like I have little left to give to my other
kids. Not to my "real" kids, but my other kids –
because they're all my real kids. They partnered
with us in obedience, and they carry some of the
weight of it with us.

*Then Moses turned to the Lord and said,
"O Lord, why have you done evil to this
people? Why did you ever send me?*

- Exodus 5:22

On those days I'm jumping behind my friend
Moses, yelling, "Yeah, what he said! What were You

thinking, sending me?" Oh, Moses, I get it. God told you to do something all radical, and you obeyed. You stood up against unrighteousness and defended the helpless. You told Pharoah to let your people go and it wasn't pretty. Bad things happened to people you loved, and they blamed you for it because they didn't hear His voice.

That was some joke, assigning a hermit-level introvert to be the mother of six kids who never stop talking. Behold, the tiny Alaskan woman, shaking her beensy widdle fist at God. The ironies abound.

I wonder if any of Moses' people really knew what was coming after the raging was over. I wonder when Moses finally believed it, for real.

They were going to be stronger, bigger.

They were going to be free, flourishing. Alive.

And Moses said to the people, "Fear not, stand firm, and see the salvation of the Lord, which He will work for you today. For the Egyptians whom you see today, you shall never see again. The Lord will fight for you, and you have only to be silent."

The Lord said to Moses, "Why do you cry to me? Tell the people of Israel to go forward."

- Exodus 14:13-15

He tells us something, too. And it, too, is personal:

Tell the people to go forward.
Prepare to be delivered.

*And the Lord went before them by day in a
pillar of cloud to lead them along the way,
and by night in a pillar of fire to give them
light, that they might travel by day and by
night. The pillar of cloud by day and the
pillar of fire by night did not depart from
before the people.*

– *Exodus 13:21-22*

I don't know what it will look like for you. I
don't even know what it'll look like for me. I know
what I *want* it to look like, but that's not really an
indicator of, you know, future performance.

*Then the angel of God who was going be-
fore the host of Israel moved and went
behind them, and the pillar of cloud moved
from before them and stood behind them,
coming between the host of Egypt and the
host of Israel.*

And there was the cloud and the darkness.

*And it lit up the night without one coming
near the other all night.*

- *Exodus 14:19-20*

We writhe in labor pains only because He is
birthing something incredible out of us. The One
who goes before us and behind us stands between
us and the enemy, and He has our back.

The smoke and fire isn't there to burn us, but
to protect us. We can stand the heat because the
sap has been running under the surface even when

we couldn't see it – and in time, the leaves start greening in all their fullness.

It's coming, and those on the ground will see it, too.

October is a special month for Alaskans. Three little letters say it all...PFD. Oh, joy!

These awesome little letters stand for Permanent Fund Dividend, and for Alaskan residents it means a certain amount (determined every year) of income per person received in October. It's not welfare, it's not public assistance, it's not money taken from taxpayers. It's income from State resources, given back to the people – because every once in a while, even the government does something brilliant.

Alaskans reapply every year. For two years we used all of ours to help cover adoption expenses, and then we took meticulous pains to make sure we applied correctly for Andrey and Reagan's first PFDs, as they were newly adopted citizens.

But in September we got two little envelopes, one for each of them. They were notices stating that despite the ream of paperwork we submitted, Andrey and Reagan were not qualified and thus would not be receiving PFDs that year. And we could appeal the decision, which may or may not be overturned, for a fee of $50.

Fiery arrows started flying toward me.

Honestly, my first thought was, Oh, expletive. And my second thought was, Wait a second. This is a bunch of hooey. God, what's going on? We did everything right, exactly the way they told us to.

He said, *Stay calm. This is only a test. Hold it high.*

So we did. It took a few days, a few emails, and a couple of phone calls, but it was all good. Just a glitch. *We're sorry. Computer error. It's all taken care of, have a nice day.*

Would it have turned out differently had we allowed fear to creep in? I think...maybe.

You know that Jesus wasn't the only one to walk on water, right? Peter did, too. Here:

> *And in the fourth watch of the night he came to them, walking on the sea. But when the disciples saw him walking on the sea, they were terrified, and said, "It is a ghost!" and they cried out in fear. But immediately Jesus spoke to them, saying, "Take heart; it is I. Do not be afraid."*
>
> *And Peter answered him, "Lord, if it is you, command me to come to you on the water." He said, "Come." So Peter got out of the boat and walked on the water and came to Jesus.*
>
> *- Matthew 14:25-29*

And then you know what happens. Or...maybe you don't. I didn't. I always thought Peter saw the waves, started to sink, freaked out, and was hauled up by Jesus.

Not so. Here we go:

> *But when he saw the wind, he was afraid, and beginning to sink he cried out, "Lord,*

save me." Jesus immediately reached out his hand and took hold of him, saying to him, "O you of little faith, why did you doubt?"

- Matthew 14:30-31

He saw the wind, and then he was afraid. And then he started to sink.

He wasn't sinking before. His fear induced the sinking. It was literally that sinking, dropping feeling.

When Peter walked on water toward Me, he was afraid of the wind. It was just a bunch of hot air.

The enemy is full of it. Hot air, I mean.

We can't hold high the shield of faith while entertaining fear at the same time. It's only one or the other, and both will cause something to happen. We have to choose.

We got another piece of paper later, from the dentist this time. After enduring seven consecutive appointments for routine maintenance that are usually covered at 100%, we received a bill. Weird. Stupid healthcare fiasco nonsense, probably.

But this time I played it cool. Called the office. Asked what the charge was for.

"Oh!" the receptionist said. "I forgot to enter the correct code. I'm so sorry. Please just disregard, you owe nothing. Have a nice day."

Shh, He said. *It's only the wind.*

The termination dust came closer down the mountains every week and the trees were just spindly silhouettes in front of pale grey sky. When snow is imminent, sweaters and scarves come out of hibernation and the heater kicks on again after being dormant for months. Thin summer jackets are stored away, replaced by puffy winter jackets stuffing the closets and taking up more than their fair share of real estate.

We usually get more windstorms than snowstorms. We're stocked with firewood, a woodstove, and a pantry full of the essentials – you know, coffee, tea, chocolate. Sometimes it's not just the wind, though. We're prepared for bigger unknowns and we know we need to be ready for emergencies, both weather and otherwise.

And can I be honest? Some of us feel like we've been living inside a passive-aggressive hurricane. Situations with our kids, our families, our country – we have high hopes, we pray hard, but we're still chilled as doubt sells us some sob-story version of our hopes and dreams. Discouragement and despair stand by, waiting, black-clothed opportunists, while their ringleader, fear, waits to dish out its poison.

There's not enough tea in the world to warm us up when these kinds of freeloaders invade our territory. Doubt, despair, fear, discouragement – they try to plunder hope from us like wind strips leaves from trees, leaving us bare, exposed, and bleak. It's the cold that creeps in when we wonder about the future.

Doubt and his ugly friends stand as shadows obscuring our vision of reality. They want us to see the job loss, but not the opportunity right around the corner. They want to show off the conflict, but not the deeper wisdom that results from it. They want to illuminate the wrinkles, but make you forget about the character and experience that came with those lines. Whatever fiction doubt tries to sell us, it's never the full story.

> *Through [Jesus] we have also obtained access by faith into this grace in which we stand, and we rejoice in hope of the glory of God.*
>
> *Not only that, but we rejoice in our sufferings, knowing that suffering produces endurance, and endurance produces character, and character produces hope, and hope does not put us to shame, because God's love has been poured into our hearts through the Holy Spirit who has been given to us.*
>
> *– Romans 5:2-5*

There's always more beneath the surface. He moves through our prayer more than we see or know. Sometimes we're stripped of leaves and comfort, but it's not because He's finished with us – it's because He has a whole new covering ready for us in the next season.

> *Therefore, my beloved brothers, be steadfast, immovable, always abounding in the work of the Lord, knowing that in the Lord your labor is not in vain.*
>
> *– 1 Corinthians 15:58*

We need His truth in circumstances that are raw, tender, and confusing, so we can know how to pray life back into them.

The truth is, sometimes we choose to walk right into the storm because we've been called on duty for a rescue operation. Other times it's because we've made a wrong turn, or it might be that we're just under attack. In any case, we have a choice to make that will affect the level of aftermath we deal with later.

He reminds me over and over: *It's not about avoiding the storm. It's about whether or not you will trust Me so I can partner with you in it.*

We can either fear the storm and its outcome, or trust the One who tells it to be still as we move with Him in the midst of it. The end of the story will be different depending on that choice. When we entertain fear, we align with it. When we entertain faith, we align with it. It's that serious.

Fear is not a feeling; it is an attack to be fought off. It is a spirit:

> *For God gave us a spirit **not of fear** but of power and love and self-control.*
>
> - 2 Timothy 1:7

Fear and worry are not the same thing as wise preparation and they will never ensure safety. In fact, they can actually grant permission to the opposite while giving us a false sense of security because we think we've thought of all the terrible potential scenarios to our situation.

It is a counterfeit that we must not fall for.

Fear knocks on our door in disguise as a security technician, when in fact he is an unrepentant criminal trespassing on our property – someone we don't want anywhere near our children. If you so much as invite fear in for tea, it will move in, take over, and rearrange your furniture. Fear is a lousy houseguest. It has terrible taste, decorating with chaos, filth, and destruction.

Do not ask for fear's opinion on things. It is a presumptuous narcissist that takes your keys and invites its friends over. And you don't like its friends. You don't want them in your house at all. So tell fear *No Soliciting*. Not now, not ever. There are good days ahead and we're not afraid of the weather.

We are to abide with God, and when we do so, His perfect love casts out fear. But here's the danger: If we're not abiding and aligning with Him, we naturally swing the other way and abide with fear.

When Peter walked on water, his fear induced chaos. He began to sink after he was afraid, not before. The fear came first.

But we're always so hard on Peter. Let's pick on someone else this time.

In the book of Isaiah, the Israelites were in a terrible storm of their own and God gave them clear instructions on what they needed to do. The problem was, they didn't like those instructions and they wanted to trust the Egyptians to save them instead.

> *"Ah, stubborn children," declares the Lord,*
> *"who carry out a plan, but not mine, and*
> *who make an alliance, but not of my Spirit,*
> *that they may add sin to sin."*
>
> *– Isaiah 30:1*

His instructions took them out of their comfort zone and they were afraid to go there. They decided to follow fear instead, trusting in false security:

> For thus said the Lord God, the Holy One of Israel, "In returning and rest you shall be saved; in quietness and in trust shall be your strength." But you were unwilling, and you said, "No! We will flee upon horses"; therefore you shall flee away; and, "We will ride upon swift steeds"; therefore your pursuers shall be swift.
>
> – Isaiah 30:15-16

He said, *Wait and listen for Me. This is your salvation and strength.* God wanted better for them:

> Therefore the Lord waits to be gracious to you, and therefore he exalts himself to show mercy to you. For the Lord is a God of justice; blessed are all those who wait for him.
>
> - Isaiah 30:18

But they said no, and their fear gave substance and permission to the phantom they were fleeing. Same song, second verse:

> Do not fear the king of Babylon, of whom you are afraid. Do not fear him, declares the Lord, for I am with you, to save you and to deliver you from his hand. I will grant you mercy, that he may have mercy on you and let you remain in your own land.

But if you say, 'We will not remain in this land,' disobeying the voice of the Lord your God and saying, 'No, we will go to the land of Egypt, where we shall not see war or hear the sound of the trumpet or be hungry for bread, and we will dwell there,' then hear the word of the Lord, O remnant of Judah. Thus says the Lord of hosts, the God of Israel: If you set your faces to enter Egypt and go to live there, **then the sword that you fear shall overtake you** *there in the land of Egypt, and* **the famine of which you are afraid shall follow close after you** *to Egypt, and there you shall die.*

- Jeremiah 42:11-16

This is serious. *Do not fear* is a command, not a suggestion, for good reason. Fear doesn't care for permission; it just wants access. The counterfeit picture of what we're afraid of may be the key that permits that access.

But agreeing with God, picturing the victory and trusting Him for what He has promised, strips the enemy of power he will wrest from us otherwise. Trusting God is the fatal, final blow that puts fear out of our misery.

We cannot use our imagination to create a picture of all the possible evils that might occur in any given situation. It's not just worrying; it's a temptation we must resist because our very lives are at stake.

The burden we carry – the light yoke – is to refuse to carry the heavy burden fear tries to place

on us. We have powerful tools not only to keep fear
from trespassing, but to dispatch it entirely:

Tell fear No Soliciting. Play it cool.

Reject anything it tries to sell you.

*Hold high the picture of victory that I've given
you.*

Hope is a powerful fuel, and when combined
with truth, it turns fear, doubt, despair, and discouragement to ashes. Our prayer is a bellows,
breathing oxygen everywhere the fire needs to be
kindled.

*Have I not commanded you? Be strong
and courageous. Do not be frightened, and
do not be dismayed, for the Lord your God
is with you wherever you go.*

- Joshua 1:9

Every night for several days in a row, I sat at
the computer and worked on a document. Then one
night I sat down to work on it some more and
couldn't find the file anywhere. So I did what any of
us might when missing a half-completed project
due in less than two weeks. I panicked.

The right file was open and I kept skimming all
the documents, checking every row and column of
titles, but it wasn't there. I started to feel this growing alarm rise in my gut.

Oh, no. Did I delete it on accident? Did the cat
walk across the keyboard and lose it? Did I in-

advertently click and drag it to some obscure file that I never use? What have I done? I imagined all sorts of things, like re-writing it, asking for an extension on the deadline, and using a sledge-hammer on an innocent laptop.

But suddenly everything seemed to come back into focus, and it was right there. It was there all along. I just hadn't recognized the new title I gave it the night before.

That same week my husband lost his wedding ring. It wasn't catastrophic; it was just a cheap replacement after the original ring had to be cut off years ago when he broke his finger. Chamberlain, however, was very concerned.

"But *Mom!*" she wailed. "If he doesn't wear his ring, *peoples is gonna try to marry him!*"

A few days later she found the ring in the bathroom by a stack of towels, saving us from impending hordes of "peoples" lined up and down our street trying to marry her daddy. He immediately rewarded her with a handful of chocolate chips.

But before that, we had one day without running water, another day when the alternator on the new vehicle went out, and another day when our beloved Sophie-cat had a seizure and we thought she was dying. All in two weeks.

I know it happens where you are, too: Emergency room visits, travel, family issues, a big move, broken bones, broken hearts, and storms (weather and otherwise) that bring unexpected aftermath.

For us, all of this came just a couple of months after ringing in the New Year with the flu, breaking a tooth, and rolling our truck off the highway in freezing rain. Exciting times. February was my favorite month that year, probably because it only had 28 days to misbehave itself.

But He is there all along in the moments of growing alarm, when I'm afraid of losing it. In the middle of the night sleeplessness, in the prayer, in the chaos of every day holding more than it feels like 24 hours rightfully should, He's right there telling us there is nothing to fear. Right there, waiting for me to focus so I can recognize Him.

In current events, in the headlines, in our family, in our uncertainty – as we are pursuing Him, He is positioning us and the events around us into specific alignment and formation.

He hasn't misplaced us. He is preparing us.

Every historic notable, every Biblical figure, every literary hero had a point when it felt like things were crashing down, when things weren't working out and were going downhill fast. They felt like they'd blown it.

In literature it's called climax, but in reality it has nothing to do with a literary formula. It is that people who lead quiet, conventional, easy lives never changed history. Epics aren't written about people who lived in mediocre normalcy.

Fear is replaced with a determination – grim, if necessary – that we are here, in this time, for a strategic purpose. That purpose is to be met, not run from and feared. We must recognize it, even if it's called a name that we had forgotten. Even if it takes us to a place we didn't expect. He's bringing things into focus to show us that He has been here all along.

Plow forward. Lean in, steady on.

He's putting us in our place...and it's a good one. It's a position of influence, of strategy, and of impact. We're not lost. We're not losing it.

We are leading.

friendship:

THE FORCE TO BE

RECKONED WITH

Five of you shall chase a hundred, and a hundred of you shall chase ten thousand, and your enemies shall fall before you by the sword.

Leviticus 26:8

Vince came home from work and handed me the mail while I was stewing on the couch, and typing and deleting on the laptop. Junk mail, junk mail, bills, donation request, political petition, junk mail – oh, happy day! My name on an envelope, in a dear friend's handwriting. *I've got mail.*

A few days later I got another letter from a different friend. And what is really amazing is that I received those letters on two nights when I was totally discouraged. Didn't want to write. Didn't want to wait or listen. Didn't want to be transparent, because what I was seeing and feeling was not flattering. Didn't want to, you can't make me, stomp and huff.

But then He sent words from friends. A gift.

You are loved, He says. *Pray without ceasing, write without quitting, and love without limits, because you need each other.*

Sometimes I am the friend who gets to give the gift. Around the same time, He gave me these words for someone: *Grasp the hope that is substantial, not airy. It has substance and weight to it.* But the words were for me, too.

I was fighting despair over a hard situation, and He reminded me that my thoughts are to look ahead and trust Him, knowing (because it is certain!) that He is making all things new and bringing life into dark places. When I believe other-wise, I'm allowing the enemy to trespass, to hinder me from obeying the truth and walking in joy.

Our hope is a real thing that has thickness and heft. It has density and can be carried. It is our calling to carry it and not give the enemy power by believing the fears he tries to put in our way.

Often, we carry it for each other. We have each other's back, because the enemy plays dirty.

Friendship is a gift with a mighty purpose, He says. *Picture the victory not just for yourselves, but for each other. Expect it.*

> *And let us not grow weary of doing good,*
> *for in due season we will reap, if we do not*
> *give up. So then, as we have opportunity,*
> *let us do good to everyone, and especially*
> *to those who are of the household of faith.*
>
> *- Galatians 6:9-10*

Hey Love, you are able to create and increase courage in each other by your words, your prayers, and your actions. Speak what is true. Pray without ceasing. Cast mountains to the sea.

So much is at stake in these small acts. They are often the aegis and covering that keeps someone from giving up before the victory comes.

I thought it would be an easy chore. Afton loves the kitchen, wants to have his hands in everything, and this seemed like the perfect task for him.

All of my flour containers were empty and they needed to be refilled from the giant bin in the pantry so I could make bread later. Easy. He was happy to tackle the mission, and I sent him off on his merry way with great confidence.

One person is powerful. We can do amazing things on our own. The prayer of a righteous (read: *devoted, pursuing God, willing to be surprised by Him*) man or woman avails much.

One of your men puts to flight a thousand,
for the LORD your God is He who fights
for you, just as He promised you.

– Joshua 23:10

I love that kind of math. But sometimes He leads us to a threshold that requires assistance to walk through. Our boots are on the ground and we need back up, stat.

Back in the kitchen twenty minutes later, Vince asked me where Afton was.

"In the pantry," I said. *Though he should have been done fifteen minutes ago. Hmm.*

"Have you seen Andrey and Reagan?"

"Um, no. I thought they were with you." Silence is golden, except when it's suspicious...

The search takes just a few seconds, brought to a firm conclusion when three (uno! dos! tres!) of the guiltiest looking seven-year-olds you ever saw slowly filed out of the pantry, covered from head to toe in flour. Just like the floor. Somehow, the one kid I sent in there multiplied into the three amigos, and their impact was (ahem) exponential.

After two years of feeding a family of eight in Alaska, we finally entered the fellowship of a bulk food co-op, which means we only have to buy things like flour every few months instead of every few weeks. It also means that our laundry room is overtaken with bags of dry goods until we figure out what to do with it all: corn masa, dried split peas, cocoa, vanilla beans, hot cereal, black beans, and a 50-pound sack of oatmeal that's about the size of a toddler bed. We'd be ready for a siege if our coffee pot wasn't still on the blink.

We should have joined years ago; I'm not sure why it took us so long. After a while, we'd heard so many endorsements from friends that we couldn't ignore it anymore. I don't usually think of myself as a follower but when a trusted friend tells me where to go to buy tea and gourmet popcorn at a fraction of the store price, I'm happy to let them lead me.

One of those dear friends called and we caught up on each other's news, big and little things, between interruptions from kiddos. We talked about puppies (hers), and kittens (ours), and paws the size of snowshoes. We commiserated over the follies of letting our children play with glitter (one of us has kids that actually had a glitter fight, and I won't name any names, but *it wasn't my kids*). We talked about church and missions, plans and weekends and prayer requests. We talked about questions we have for the future, about answers we're waiting for, and about wanting those answers, as long as we get to pick and choose what they are. And she stopped me and prayed right then. She was telling me where to go again, and it was exactly what I needed.

> *Then Joshua rose early in the morning and they set out from Shittim. And they came to the Jordan, he and all the people of Israel, and lodged there before they passed over. At the end of three days the officers*

went through the camp and commanded the people, **"As soon as you see the ark of the covenant of the Lord your God being carried by the Levitical priests, then you shall set out from your place and follow it."**

– Joshua 3:1-3

Sometimes our obedience and boldness are the signs God has placed for someone else to see. At such a time as this, our willingness may be what they are watching for.

"For the Lord your God dried up the waters of the Jordan for you until you passed over, as the Lord your God did to the Red Sea, which he dried up for us until we passed over, **so that all the peoples of the earth may know** *that the hand of the Lord is mighty, that you may fear the Lord your God forever."*

– Joshua 4:23-24

Friendship rooted in prayer, challenging us to obedience, is a powerful force to be reckoned with. The enemy takes notice and shrinks back:

As soon as all the kings of the Amorites who were beyond the Jordan to the west, and all the kings of the Canaanites who were by the sea, heard that the Lord had dried up the waters of the Jordan for the people of Israel until they had crossed over, **their hearts melted and there was no longer any spirit in them**

because of the people of Israel.

— Joshua 5:1

We need each other. A united front creates a force to be reckoned with.

You need to pray for each other, He says. *It is your greatest weapon against darkness and your greatest defense against the enemy. You need to pray with and for each other as much as possible, prayer that goes deep and wide and perhaps unnoticed by the recipient, but altogether effective nonetheless.*

You need to show grace to each other and trust that I am speaking to each of you. Your effectiveness diminishes in proportion to your friendly fire.

I've called you to increase courage in each other because you will need it. If you are not speaking life and victory over each other, you are in retreat.

When you are united, your impact is exponential. This is where you find the victory.

And this friend and I, when we met over ten years ago, I was her leader — but as the years passed and our friendship grew, we took turns leading, guiding, and counseling. It's a beautiful back-and-forth, as two leaders listen and learn from each other's influence.

These friends are the ones we go to battle with. They're also the ones we go to battle for. And if you find one who understands why you get heart palpitations over glitter, well...that one's a keeper.

We walked to the mailbox in brisk wind, and came home to warm clothes in the dryer and several more loads on deck. I sorted mail and hauled an armload of clothes to the living room couch to be folded, but from across the room I heard the dryer door opening and slamming shut repeatedly.

I peeked around the corner. Chamberlain had the junk mail I just gave her, and she threw it in the dryer. *Slam.* Open the door, take out the mail. *Slam.* Repeat.

"Hey, Cham, what are you doing?"

"Checking my mailbox." *SLAM!*

"Oh." Four-year-olds are geniuses. "Well, I need to flip the laundry and you're going to have to find something else to be your mailbox. Sorry."

She looks toward the kitchen and doesn't miss a beat. "Like the oven?"

She is a sharp, fast thinker. Fearless, too, with a mighty future ahead. She has amazing assets. Someday they will all come in handy, and hopefully won't involve any structure fires or broken appliances.

*"Let me tell you what's been going on −"
He stopped and shook his head. "No," he said. "There's too much, it would take too long, let me distill it for you: the wedding is at six, which leaves us probably now something over half an hour to get in, steal the girl, and get out; but not before I kill Count Rugen."*

"What are our liabilities?"

"There is but one working castle gate and

it is guarded by perhaps a hundred men."

"Hmmm," Westley said, not as unhappy as he might have been ordinarily, because just then he began to be able to wiggle his toes.

"And our assets?"

"Your brains, Fezzik's strength, my steel."

- William Goldman [1]

Brains, strength, steel. I need more of each. It is weeks, months since we wrote that list and agreed to walk through the threshold, and I'm still unsure about how to tackle everything in the big picture.

I'll give you everything you need, He says. *It won't always be what you expect.*

Often, I'll give it to you in the form of other people. Otherwise you would think you could do it all on your own, and eventually, you would think you could do it without Me.

I'm putting just the right people in your path to walk with you, He says. *I'm also putting you in the path of others, to walk with them. But hey, Love...do not always expect a leisurely stroll to the mailbox.*

It is a serious indication of a most desperate need for coffee when in the process of making it, you realize that you almost forgot to put in the filter.

It was one of those days: a late bedtime followed by an early morning, slogging around the house Neanderthal-style, dragging my feet and bumping into walls, just barely coasting into the weekend only to collapse on the couch when Vin got home from work.

I'd like to say it was due to something altruistic or noble, but no. It was the result of a cat who appointed himself as the family alarm clock, combined with the unforgiving effects of a late-night writing hangover.

Only four hours after I'd hit "publish" the night before, the cat went off. He has no snooze button, no volume control; he just howls until his battery runs down and then comes back to bed, arranging himself on my feet, utterly shameless.

Usually he's still sleeping there when I get up. Usually I gently make the bed around him, slowly pulling the blankets straight underneath him, because I'm a softie, probably still in the running for the title of Crazy Cat Lady despite my married status.

But on this day, I wasn't a softie. I yanked the covers straight and sent him spinning a little.

Sophie (who, on this morning, we'll call *the good cat*) was on my heels to the bathroom. You know it's been a rough night when you're brushing your teeth and look over, and even your cat has that no-makeup-I-need-my-coffee look.

The whole day of schooling and feeding and caring for six children was ahead of me, and something jogged my memory during breakfast. I read about a situation just like this recently. What was it? Something about...Churchill, I think...in his escape from prison during the Boer War...ah, yes.

Here we go:

> *Armed only with seventy-four pounds sterling, four slabs of chocolate, and a few biscuits, [Churchill] faced three hundred miles of hostile territory populated by people whose language he did not understand.*
>
> - Stephen Mansfield [2]

Exactly. This describes the day of mothering ahead of me with eerie precision.

Yet somehow the hours pass and we all survive. Kids are fed, taught, kissed and tucked in bed. Copious amounts of chocolate and coffee are consumed.

That night, I sit at the computer and try to think. Try to pray. Try to listen. Try to write. But what I really want to do is browse the internet, or read a book, or sleep.

Vince walks past on his way to the kitchen. "How's it going?"

I tell him I'm tired. I tell him I have three sentences that I've deleted three times. I tell him I need to go to bed by 1 am and I still haven't showered. And I think I have nothing to write.

"You're at mile twenty," he said.

I look at him, bleary and impatient. "What?"

"Like in a marathon. You've hit the wall, you want to quit. Just get past this and you'll pick up speed again."

I snort, or grunt, or something. I hate running. Running is for people who enjoy pain and don't care about breathing so much. And I don't have time for conversation. I have to write something.

But the quiet voice I'm trying to ignore tells me that God is speaking through him – not because He's not speaking to me, but because I'm not listening very well to either of them and I need a more audible voice.

He is a patient man. A good husband. His tone is gentle and not condemning, reflecting the voice of both the Father and the husband who love me. And He's aware of something I've lost sight of and knows I need perspective.

He ignores my withering looks and quietly says something that I don't suggest many husbands say to their wives. He is allowed to, though, since he keeps better track of these things than I do.

"Also, you're ovulating."

Oh. That makes sense.

Suddenly the day behind me is described with eerie precision. A weight is lifted, and I no longer feel entirely responsible for how sluggish I've felt all day. I know I'll pick up speed again tomorrow. His mercy will greet me in the morning, whether or not the cat goes off too early. And I still have a few slabs of chocolate left.

Blessed be the God and Father of our Lord Jesus Christ, the Father of mercies and God of all comfort, who comforts us in all our affliction, so that we may be able to comfort those who are in any affliction,

*with the comfort with which we ourselves
are comforted by God.*

- 2 Corinthians 1:3-4

It was dangerous, full of chaos and screaming. Time was short and I had to fly.

I ran upstairs, down the hall, and into the bedroom, turning the doorknob with care so the latch would be silent. Tiptoed behind the bed, knelt to the floor, and prayed.

Hide me, I whispered. For a minute, all was quiet and my heart slowed down. I thought for sure I was being followed. A blanket was on the floor and I wrapped myself in a cocoon, wondering what was happening downstairs.

The door shook with sudden, intense pounding. They found me.

"Mo-ooom! Can we come in? We know you're in there!" Game over.

It's not always for fun, though—usually I'm up here several times a day seeking a minute of peace and quiet in the middle of the craziness, or hiding in the pantry for a while to think and regroup. With kids misbehaving, hormones raging, and laundry piling, I need to hide in Him. I have to run to the bivouac often so I can be effective back in the battle. His presence is mandatory; chocolate chips are optional.

I am the vine; you are the branches. Whoever abides in me and I in him, he it is that bears much fruit, for apart from me you can do nothing.

- John 15:5

We know this verse so well it threatens to numb us in familiarity. We know that we bear fruit when we abide in his presence. We pay so much attention to this that sometimes we overlook the other role of branches that are connected to the vine: they are a covering for those who seek refuge.

We run to him, the Vine, so we can be His hands and feet to others when they come to us. Branches are a shelter and the vulnerable run to them for protection. They provide safety and offer crucial cover for small creatures seeking sanctuary from predators. It's where they build nests, give birth to new life, and raise their families. Particularly for moths and butterflies, the branches are a haven where they cocoon and then transform into what He made them to be.

We are that for others, they are that for us. Friends, family, church, and home are the emotional shelters we cultivate for each other — these are the relationships where we nurse our wounds and rest after a hard day. They're the school that teaches and grows us, and sometimes, they're our emergency room.

It's not a tangible place, but a spiritual safety we create for others in our relationships. It is where love is tended and fruit is borne. It is where life is protected.

It sounds a lot like motherhood and ministry. Maybe that's why mothers and ministers need to pay extra-close attention to their need for refuge when their tank begins to empty — we focus so much on providing shelter for others that often we forget that we need to seek sanctuary too.

Sometimes we get lost in the wilderness. And He is our refuge, of course — but in His abundant

generosity, He also gives us friends to confirm His
wisdom and to comfort us as we navigate the dark
forest.

> *Oh, how abundant is your goodness, which*
> *you have stored up for those who fear you*
> *and worked for those who take refuge in*
> *you, in the sight of the children of man-*
> *kind!*
>
> *In the cover of your presence you hide*
> *them from the plots of men; you store them*
> *in your shelter from the strife of tongues.*

- Psalm 31:19-20

For over two years I went through a dark
season, plowing through expectations, obligations,
the feeling of never doing enough, never being
enough, and not having the time or emotional mar-
gin to do more than walk around in circles. I knew
that grace was there, but I couldn't see it; I knew
that I was supposed to feel free, but instead I felt
fried.

But my friends could see it for me. Those
closest to me spoke freedom into me when I didn't
have the words for myself.

The predator was always out there with his lies
and accusations. One afternoon I ran upstairs for a
quick break from the chores, discipline, schooling,
cooking, and bickering – I was burned out and
knew it, and thought I would take a few minutes to
journal some of it out. Before I even found my pen,
I was fighting the guilt and accusations with
thoughts like, *What's wrong with me? It's ridi-*

*culous to feel this way. How ungrateful of me, how
negative, blah-blah-blah —*

But my thoughts were interrupted by one boy
wailing and two girls arguing outside my door. They
wanted in, of course. And I thought, *No wonder I'd
rather hide in a corner and write sometimes.*

I let them come in, provided a safe place, and
helped them sort out their conflict. And then I fled
for comfort, too. After Vince got home, I went out
with a friend and we discovered we were wandering
through the same dark forest.

We caught up over onion rings and shakes and
shared our stories. We talked about recipes for little
boys who won't eat chicken, consequences for kids
caught lying, and the effort put into staying up late
and getting up early to meet deadlines. We grieved
over the catch-22 of always feeling like we're doing
too much and yet never getting enough done.

The same wolf was chasing both of us, but it
took the shelter of each other's perspective to iden-
tify his tracks. Together we recognized the traps
he'd been setting, and our friendship restocked the
ammo we needed to fight back.

> *In the embracing light and warmth, warm
> and dry at last, with weary legs propped
> up in front of them, and a suggestive clink
> of plates being arranged on the table be-
> hind, it seemed to the storm-driven ani-
> mals, now in safe anchorage, that the cold
> and trackless Wild Wood just left outside
> was miles and miles away, and all that
> they had suffered in it a half-forgotten
> dream.*
>
> *- Kenneth Grahame* 3

From that thicket of safety we wiped crumbs and tears and moved on to easier topics, like movies, music lessons, and nosy phone solicitors. We snickered over the irony of surveys that ask about our children's consumption of soft drinks when we don't buy soda. We comforted each other with the fact that while we aren't perfect parents, at least we could console ourselves with the knowledge that we don't put Rockstar in our kids' sippy cups. A little perspective does wonders.

We need each other's point of view so we can have each other's back. Through our prayers, our friendship, and our words, we shield those around us from harm. We comfort them when they're hurting and create a safe place to rest and grow as they seek Him. Our friendships are the haven, the hospice, and occasionally the theater that provides comic relief and satire after a hard day.

He made us to be a covering for each other.

We don't stay there constantly. There's a whole forest to be tended, loved, and known as we reach out to provide the comfort He gives us to the communities around us. Sometimes we're the temporary hostel for acquaintances and strangers just passing through. Other times we're the chapel.

But we do come back to our own nest in the bracken — these close relationships that nurture us — to rest, reassess, and recuperate.

> *He did not at all want to abandon the new life and its splendid spaces, to turn his back on sun and air and all they offered him and creep home and stay there; the upper world was all too strong, it called to him still, even down there, and he knew he*

must return to the larger stage. But it was
good to think he had this to come back to,
this place which was all his own, these
things which were so glad to see him again
and could always be counted upon for the
same simple welcome.

- Kenneth Grahame [4]

We are His hands and feet when we comfort our crying child, our hurting friend, and the weeping stranger. We give cover to those under attack whether they are bullied at school, scapegoated at work, or overseas in the battle, desperately in need of prayer at the exact moment God brings them to mind. He calls us to be the rescue mission, the special ops team, the trauma center that reaches out to others who seek His sanctuary.

He allows us to provide from far-off when we scatter seed by the wind, sending our support and prayer to those far away. And He is there, too, unleashing protection and provision over them in places our own roots may never reach.

These relationships are the cocoon in our daily lives and in crisis. We hide there in His protection as we walk with each other through metamorphosis and change, from death to life. We are meant to fly together.

fire:

ATTACK, OVERWHELM,

AND INTERCESSION

For our struggle is not against flesh and blood, but against the rulers, against the authorities, against the powers of this dark world and against the spiritual forces of evil in the heavenly realms. Therefore put on the full armor of God, so that when the day of evil comes, you may be able to stand your ground, and after you have done everything, to stand.

Ephesians 6:12-13

Confession time, housewife edition: I don't do spring cleaning, I don't rearrange furniture for fun, and I don't overhaul closets in the fall. Those are deceptive, sneaky projects.

In the attempt to take them on, you make a bigger mess than you had in the first place and there's no end to it. You tackle one simple thing like de-cluttering a few kitchen cabinets, and suddenly you're surrounded by lidless jars you have to box up for the recycling center, unused gadgets to donate to the thrift store, unidentifiable spices that lost their aroma sometime before Y2K, and a depression-era bottle of corn syrup permanently cemented to the back of the shelf.

I know these things need to be taken care of, but so much is already on my plate. The piano needs tuned, the chimney needs swept, the septic needs pumped – just keeping it real, folks – and it's hard enough to remember to refill prescriptions on time. I'm not venturing into the kitchen cabinets until at least May.

If it were just making phone calls and running errands it wouldn't be so daunting, but those tasks compound with bigger, more complicated things, like appointments that take more out of you than a $150 fee. Situations intensify and loom over us, requiring more than elbow grease and a checkbook to finish off.

This kind of stuff doesn't fit neatly on a to-do list: Hard relationships. Hard decisions. Health issues, deadlines, changes, and clutter. You know the ones – those things that float around, making mental noise and disorder. They're not even all bad; mostly, they're just taking up far more space than any one situation rightfully should, like a two-year-old with a mocha. It's not that the concerns aren't real or don't need to be addressed. But stacked on top of each other, they magnify way out of proportion from stress, exhaustion, and fear. Negative words from within and without cast each issue on the wall in an intimidating shadow, a projected image that is much bigger than what reality actually deals us.

Sometimes my kids' special needs make my head spin. Also – maybe you've heard of this? – there are seasons when stars collide and families experience the amazing hormonal trifecta of adolescence, PMS, and menopause in all of its explosive awesomeness. I've, um, heard it happens. Some places.

Instead of grasping at all these issues out of my reach, He's teaching me to bring them down to earth where I can put them under authority and see them for what they are.

I'm learning to nail them down. I just use my old journal, but I don't think you don't have to be a writer to do this.

The stress, sickness, chaos, and deadlines get filtered onto the paper, one thing at a time. As I write each thing down, big and small, they're caught and pinned. They might squirm a little but they're not going anywhere, and I can look them in the eye and rest again. And when I read it later (in admittedly awful handwriting) they're all brought down, down, down to the right size.

It's completely honest, nothing fancy. Pure, rough, unrefined, like the tree that He nailed everything to 2000 years ago. It is us, hushed, listening for Him. It is praying on paper. He speaks when we listen, and for me, the clutter is quieter and He is louder when I write it out. The Spirit falls and the Son is magnified. All those issues come down a peg, brought down to size before the One who really knows what to do about all of it.

It's significant that paper is made from the same material He was nailed to. He still uses it to heal us, show us more of Him, and conquer what's harassing us.

He is not afraid of bad news; his heart is firm, trusting in the Lord. His heart is steady; he will not be afraid, until he looks in triumph on his adversaries.

- Psalm 112:7-8

Our usual response when we come under attack is to pray directly for the situation. If we get sick, we pray to get better. If we're struggling with finances, we pray for provision. If we're in a hard relationship, we pray for wisdom and healing. It makes sense. Of course we want to strike back at the same place the enemy is attacking.

But when we deal with spiritual attack from spiritual enemies (whether they're working through humans or something else entirely) sometimes the obvious answer doesn't always work; it seems to persist no matter how much or often we strike it with prayer.

A while ago a friend shared a strategy I'd never heard of, called "prayer trigger, prayer target." It made no sense at all to me at first: You experience attack in one area, and you respond not by praying for that, but by choosing something completely unrelated to intercede for every time it happens. Something big. Just a quick prayer, steadily fired, each time you deal with that attack.

Weird, hmm? Sort of a different tack on "resist the enemy and he will flee from you" – play it cool and use it as a reminder to intercede in a big way. So I tried it. And as weeks went by, I saw huge moves in both the area I was praying for and in the area I was attacked in.

I also found a possible explanation for it.

[Jesus] went away from there and came to his hometown, and his disciples followed him. And on the Sabbath he began to teach in the synagogue, and many who heard him were astonished, saying, "Where did this man get these things? What is the wisdom given to him? How are such mighty works done by his hands?

Is not this the carpenter, the son of Mary and brother of James and Joses and Judas and Simon? And are not his sisters here with us?" And they took offense at him.

And Jesus said to them, "A prophet is not without honor, except in his hometown and among his relatives and in his own household." And he could do no mighty work there, except that he laid his hands on a few sick people and healed them. And he marveled because of their unbelief.

- Mark 6:1-6a

The people in Jesus' hometown thought they knew who He was, but what they thought they knew tripped them up from knowing what they really needed to know. You can't teach know-it-alls who are confident in their own ignorance.

Luke's account tells us more. Right before the people asked, "Hey, isn't this Joseph's son?" this happened:

> *And he rolled up the scroll and gave it back to the attendant and sat down. And the eyes of all in the synagogue were fixed on him. And he began to say to them, "Today this Scripture has been fulfilled in your hearing."* **And all spoke well of him and marveled at the gracious words that were coming from his mouth.** *And they said, "Is not this Joseph's son?"*

- Luke 4:20-22

They were perfectly happy with His good news until they realized, *Wait a second – don't we know this guy? Who does he think he is?* Their assumption of familiarity and proximity was a handicap to their belief.

I never understood Jesus' response to them until I made the connection with this. Here's what He said:

> *And he said, "Truly, I say to you, no prophet is acceptable in his hometown. But in truth, I tell you,* **there were many**

*widows in Israel in the days of Elijah,
when the heavens were shut up three years
and six months, and a great famine
came over all the land, and Elijah
was sent to none of them but only to
Zarephath, in the land of Sidon, to a
woman who was a widow. And there
were many lepers in Israel in the time
of the prophet Elisha, and none of them
was cleansed, but only Naaman the
Syrian."*

- Luke 4:24-27

Jesus wasn't the first person to be doubted or rejected. Both Elijah and Elisha carried power, but they were both sent to unfamiliar people and places during those times to bless others with it.

So, back to praying about attack. If we're honest with ourselves, is it possible that our familiarity with our own stuff – our own relationships, our own health issues, whatever it is – might sometimes hinder our belief in God's ability to heal or bring restoration to it? We're too close; we know too much. We know the pain and the pain is loud. We know how complex and impossible the situation is. We've prayed before but still haven't experienced victory.

This is why we ask others to pray for us, right? We can often believe bigger for each other than we can for ourselves – it's easier to believe in miracles for others when we're not sidelined by the raw pain of it all.

It's also why going on the offense to pray for something completely unrelated might be more effective than fretting to God about our problem and calling it prayer.

It could be that we're continuing to pray for our circumstances not out of belief, but out of unbelief. Do we really believe God heard us? It still hurts, it's still broken, so do we really trust that He is already taking care of it? Or are we the child who was already given a favorable answer but keeps coming back to ask the same question over and over anyway, not believing their parent is really going to follow through?

It's true that sometimes we need to continue to pray for a particular situation; Jesus prayed twice for a man to receive his sight. You might also remember that He told the parable of a persistent widow knocking repeatedly at a judge's door for justice – which many apply as reason to continue in prayer, though it's actually a contrast between an unrighteous judge who eventually listens to the woman out of frustration, versus God our Father speedily giving "justice to His elect who cry out to Him day and night."

> *I tell you, he will give justice to them speedily. Nevertheless, when the Son of Man comes, will he find faith on earth?*
>
> *- Luke 18:8*

We might need to keep praying. But we also need to examine our hearts to see if we're continuing to pray the same thing because we need to, or if it's because we don't trust Him to answer us in the first place.

It might be that we need to just thank Him for hearing and answering us, because He repeatedly tells us He will.[1] It might be that once we've prayed about it, we need to trust Him to move beyond what we can see and then go on to pray for other things.

Search me, O God, and know my heart!
Try me and know my thoughts!

- Psalm 139:23

What we think we know can get in the way of what we need to know – and what we need to know is that God is big enough to take care of this situation and bring total redemption to it.

In the meantime, we can believe for wild healing and restoration for someone else, and watch Him move on behalf of both of us. Our victory is here.

It took two and a half years, but I finally finished reading *Les Miserables* (insert wild, nerdy rejoicing). In it, I read about a major cleanup operation – the saturated underground sewer system in Paris.

It was a formidable campaign;
a nocturnal battle against pestilence and
suffocation. [2]

Trust me, it's safe, nothing graphic. Let's keep going.

The operation was complicated; the visit
entailed the necessity of cleaning; hence it
was necessary to cleanse and at the same

time, to proceed...They advanced with toil.
The lanterns pined away in the foul
atmosphere. From time to time, a fainting
sewerman was carried out. [3]

Still with me? One more little section:

At certain points, there were precipices.
The soil had given away, the pavement
had crumbled, the sewer had changed into
a bottomless well; they found nothing
solid; a man disappeared suddenly; they
had great difficulty in getting him out
again. [4]

The project was tackled in 1805 because one
man was willing to go into the putrid darkness and
do something about it.

His name was Pierre Bruneseau. He did what
needed to be done in the place and time he lived in,
willing to be the cleanup operation and go into the
dark when others shuddered at the thought of it.

God nudged me as I read it. What would happen if each of us took this approach with prayer?

What would happen if those darkest, most
hopeless places, institutions, and people were tackled in prayer on a level that no one has had the grit
and persistence to take on before?

What if we prayed – *really* prayed, with bright,
life-giving detail – over those who've grown wild,
refusing to admit fault, admit reality, admit their
own weakness? What if we were brave enough to
picture what it would look like if the darkest
businesses were replaced with those that breathed
life in a community – and then we prayed it into
existence?

A friend said this in a sermon and it stuck with me: *The presence of fire in the Bible often symbolizes the presence of God.* The fire on the mountain, the burning bush, the pillar of smoke, the tongues of fire that could not be contained in a room.

His presence sanctifies, purifies, covers, and brings light.

*Therefore let us be grateful for receiving a kingdom that cannot be shaken, and thus let us offer to God acceptable worship, with reverence and awe, **for our God is a consuming fire**.*

- Hebrews 12:28-29

The light yoke of responsibility, maturity, and surrender are only a breath away. The heavy yoke of filth and blackness costs so much, and lies to those who are in it that the effort to take the deep breath of surrender isn't worth it. What if we made the road smoother through prayer that refuses to give up on them?

I've also been the one who was lost, and losing, and needed someone to fight in prayer for me. Many of us would not be who we are today without those who fought the darkness for us.

We have loved ones stuck in this kind of mire, and this is where the fight comes in for those of us who love them and are tempted to just wash our hands and give up on them. Giving up seems easier to us, just as it seems to them, because the pain of disappointment after raised hopes is so hard to bear.

But this stubborn, unyielding prayer is where we fight, because the decision between hope and despair is where the battle rages. This is where the outcome of victory or defeat is decided. And we should take someone with us, because even spiritual proximity to the morass can threaten to suck us under, too. We can be the powerful loving ones, clinging to a healthy vision of the one who is lost in darkness, refusing to let it go.

> *Be sober-minded; be watchful. Your adversary the devil prowls around like a roaring lion, seeking someone to devour. Resist him, firm in your faith, knowing that the same kinds of suffering are being experienced by your brotherhood throughout the world.*
>
> *- 1 Peter 5:8-9*

We cling to this hope and pray it into existence regardless of the blackness that pulses and threatens. We could fade away and give up, but heroes run into the battle and not away from it. Our loved ones need us to be those heroes – because they too are meant to be heroes, and that's why the enemy fights so desperately for them.

That enemy whispers, "Give up. Lower your weapons."

And we respond, "Fire."

The wind, it is a-whipping. Leaves fly upward in the face of gravity and past the empty trees they fell from. The color outside is ashen and faded like an old photo.

The clock, it is a-ticking. We sail toward bedtime and six kids are almost in jammies, but the littlest sister is teasing the oldest brother about wearing polka dots. It turns into a wonderful teaching moment about 1) getting dressed when Mommy says so, 2) being patient with younger siblings, 3) not harassing each other, and 4) the difference between polka dots and camo, which is what he was really wearing.

They all troop into the bathroom to brush teeth, and it starts with gagging and sputtering because someone put soap on the toothbrushes again. A quick sniff to find the one toothbrush that does not smell like soap confirms the perpetrator, who has done this trick off and on for two years now. Everyone's toothbrush gets rinsed, the culprit's toothbrush gets graced with a taste of the soap he intended to inflict on others, and everyone brushes.

One of these days he'll learn these antics aren't necessary. He'll learn he doesn't have to protect himself with spikes and thorns because he'll know he has a far grander purpose in life. He wasn't meant to live in fear; he wasn't meant to give into temptations from old habits and false identity; he was meant to be a warrior.

Therefore take up the whole armor of God, that you may be able to withstand in the evil day, and having done all, to stand firm. Stand therefore, having fastened on the belt of truth, and having put on the breastplate of righteousness, and, as shoes for your feet, having put on the readiness given by the gospel of peace.

– Ephesians 6:13-15

Sometimes it's all I can do just to keep our kids from throwing toys at each other or sabotaging each other's toothbrushes; I struggle to wrap my mind around the bigger, broader issues outside our door. And I even feel guilty for praying for comparatively small needs in our home when there are immensely huge events happening out there.

It feels urgent, like we have to choose – and what if something tragic is happening to issue B while I'm still praying over issue A?

That's just me. You are probably far more calm and level-headed about all this.

I catch myself slipping into this different kind of fear, an anxiety over prayer – which is ridiculous, since that's the opposite of what prayer should accomplish – and it takes me a while to realize that it's just another ploy of the enemy to make something productive and powerful seem burdensome and impotent.

And that's a lie. The enemy is a liar who is afraid of God's people praying. He will do whatever he can to convince us not to do it, which is a very good reason to do it without ceasing.

Like most lies and doubts, the lie that states our prayer isn't powerful enough, or fast enough, or covering enough is a half-truth. It's true that terrible things happen all over the world and we can't possibly pray over everything at once with the proper urgency to pick them all off one at a time, as though we were playing some sort of spiritual Galaga.

But it is also true that you and I don't have to think of everything or be in control of everything. This fear and anxiety is not all that different from what causes my son to sabotage and give up on his relationships with his family – both stem from an unhealthy need for control and a distrust in the One in authority to be able to handle the hard things within and around us. Like a good parent, we can trust God to teach us to listen for and obey His promptings, and we can trust Him to deal with everything we can't take care of at any given moment.

Because it is also true that God is not limited to our time frame.

> *If you picture Time as a straight line along which we have to travel, then you must picture God as the whole page on which the line is drawn. We come to the parts of the line one by one: we have to leave A behind before we get to B, and cannot reach C until we leave B behind. God, from above or outside or all round, contains the whole line, and sees it all.*
>
> *– C.S. Lewis* 5

Being filled with truth, knowing we are covered by Jesus' righteousness, protects us from fear and anxiety. Once we disarm fear with faith, we can go anywhere in prayer He calls us. We move from defense to offense and follow the promptings He gives us.

> *In all circumstances take up the shield of faith, with which you can extinguish all the flaming darts of the evil one; and take the helmet of salvation, and the sword of the Spirit, which is the word of God, praying at all times in the Spirit, with all prayer*

and supplication.

– Ephesians 6:16-18a

As we pursue prayer in the offhand moments, He teaches us to notice things we never would have on our own. We look out the window and instead of just staring at the leaves whipping across the street, we intercede for the neighbor who lives there. We watch the leaves shoot upward and we pray for her house, her safety, her warmth through the winter. We pray for the neighbors to be kind, patient, and gracious to each other. We pray for a sense of community, respect, and camaraderie. And there goes the neighborhood.

Our countries are in dire need of Jesus. Our leaders need wisdom and repentance just like we do, our towns and cities need protection just like our homes, businesses, churches, and schools do – and we can pray for any of them without fearing that we're missing something urgent to avoid tragedy.

Our nations are at a pivotal moment, and our prayers for small things and big things make a difference. He hears and moves because prayer is powerful and productive. Years from now, we will look back on these days and know that we saved lives and slew monsters through relentless intercession.

To that end keep alert with all perseverance, making supplication for all the saints, and also for me, that words may be given to me in opening my mouth boldly to proclaim the mystery of the gospel, for which I am an ambassador in chains, that

I may declare it boldly, as I ought to speak.

– Ephesians 6:18b-20

Relentless prayer makes for courageous people. We were never meant to live in fear. We were meant to be warriors...even if you wear polka dots. I mean, camo.

I woke to the sound of dripping again. It was still dark outside; at first I didn't recognize the steady *thp thp thp thp*, and in my groggy stupor I couldn't tell if it was coming from inside or outside. It took me a minute before I remembered and realized He was telling me to pray. Right then, for something immediate.

I started to ask Him what to pray for, but before I could even think the question He interrupted me with His answer: *For America*. The clock said 6:46, and I rolled out of bed to go turn off the water.

On the way to the bathroom I started praying for the usual suspects and wondered if headlines were already happening. You know which ones – the headlines we dread, the ones we remember from 9/11, the ones we never want to see again. And I prayed they wouldn't. We never want to wake up to headlines that break hearts again.

And we didn't – not here, not that day, at least. Not on our watch, as we pray His words over our cities.

In the beginning was the Word, and the Word was with God, and the Word was

*God. He was in the beginning with God. All
things were made through him, and without him was not any thing made that was
made. In him was life, and the life was the
light of men.*

— John 1:1-4

He tells us to pray in ways that simultaneously
prevent events from happening and create things
into being.

We are learning the relentless, without-ceasing
part: During a sermon, interceding for the pastor
and our hearts as we listen; during conversation,
changing a one-on-one discussion into a conference
call with God, whether the other person knows it or
not; during our reading and study as we talk to God
about the words on the page and discern whether or
not they align with truth.

*The light shines in the darkness, and the
darkness has not overcome it.*

— John 1:5

Throughout the day we're praying, and not just
in the quiet available moments. During laundry,
during the commute, during the phone call with the
specialist – we're asking, *Lord, what are Your
words here?* And He's right there, waking us up to
bring light into dark places. We get to help make
the headlines, and lights are turning on everywhere.

light:

TRANSFORMING CULTURE

BY RADIATING JESUS

But God does not call his people simply to run around putting out fires after the secular world has lighted them. He calls us to light our own fires, to renew culture.

Charles Colson [1]

When we moved here, this was a big house to us. Not huge – we went down from four bedrooms to three bedrooms, but that was okay because we gained a few hundred square feet and a garage. Plus an acre of woods. Plus, we left the city for the country, which meant not hearing sirens, neighbors arguing, or the booming bass and scratching speakers of young drivers who had poor manners and equally bad hearing.

Three more kids and two more cats later, we still love our home, and we still fit in it, but it's a tighter fit than when we first came. When someone plays the piano, you hear it in every room of the house. There are scratches on the floor, we've patched holes in the walls, and the rooms shrunk to make way for more people and more bookshelves. It's far more shabby chic than showy contemporary.

> *Whatever you do, work heartily, as for the Lord and not for men, knowing that from the Lord you will receive the inheritance as your reward. You are serving the Lord Christ.*
>
> *– Colossians 3:23-24*

And I'm learning to pray that God would be cleaning us as I clean the house. As I'm scrubbing grime around the sink faucets, I'm asking Him to remove calcified areas and hardening stubbornness. Dusting neglected areas, I'm asking Him to reveal what needs attention and care. Folding towels, I'm thanking Him for clean water and healthy bodies, and praying for those who have neither. While sorting boy clothes on one side of the couch and girl clothes on the other, I'm praying that these kids would be grateful for what they have, steward their things well, and not be immature whiners. And I'm praying that for me, too.

Our relentless prayer is behind the scenes, life-transforming, future-changing, people-saving work, but it's not glittering and sophisticated. It's rugged, rustic, primitive − beautiful in humility, sincerity, and imperfection. It is the movement underground that builds until the earth shakes.

It's not just requests and intercession. It's not just praise and thankfulness. Mostly, it's His presence encompassing every type of prayer, like music that permeates every room of a house.

> *It is not what I say; it is I, Myself. It is not the hearing Me so much as the being in My Presence. The strengthening and curative powers of this you cannot know. Such knowledge is beyond your human reckoning.*

> *This would cure the poor sick world, if every day, each soul, or group of souls, waited before Me. Remember, you must never fail to keep this time apart with Me.* **Gradually you will be transformed,** *physically, mentally, spiritually, into My likeness. All who see you, or contact with you will be, by this intercourse with you, brought near to Me, and gradually the influence will spread.*

> *You are making one spot of earth a Holy*

*Place, and though you must work and
spend yourself ceaselessly because that is
for the present your appointed task, yet the
greatest work either of you can do, and are
doing, is done in this time apart with Me.* ²

It doesn't matter if we go from the kitchen to
the office, or from interceding to just waiting to
hear His voice – the Music is there, filling every
room.

The moon is full, the woods behind the house
are silver. Six kids are in jammies with their teeth
brushed – without soap this time – all ready for
bed. I call them to the window.

"Look at the moon!" They stampede to admire
it, climbing on the couch cushions for a better view.
Their breath fogs the glass in front of them,
somewhat defeating the purpose of crowding so
close to the window.

Our littlest one is a four-year-old dumpling,
bouncing in her excitement.

"Mom! There's two moons!"

"Nope, there's just one."

"No, two!" She points outside, near the trees.
"Right there!"

I smile. "That's a streetlight."

"Oh," she says, but she's not too disappointed
since her enthusiasm gave her a brief chance to
jump on the couch. She's full, she's warm, she's
happy; she's off to bed and armed with a little more
knowledge than she had a minute ago.

Correcting, teaching, and answering their questions all day long is exhausting. It took me years to learn – and I'm still learning – that I won't get a simple, accepting response of "oh" or "okay" if my answers sound annoyed, exasperated, or superior.

We talk with our kids all day long for good reason. Every conversation we engage in changes or maintains the atmosphere of our home, office, ministry, and community, for better or worse. Whatever the season or temperature outside, the way we speak determines if it's warm or cool inside. Our words and tone keep us close to each other or push us apart.

Our conversations can leave others full or empty, in rain or shine.

> *Let your speech always be gracious, seasoned with salt, so that you may know how you ought to answer each person.*
>
> *- Colossians 4:6*

It's not always easy. Life is messy, full of tough situations and emotional topics that require heaps of wisdom and self-control in order to keep our conversations filled with grace. Like reproduction. Like divorce. Like...arithmetic. You know it's true.

My son is in second grade and he's learning to add large numbers together. He understands tens, hundreds, and thousands, no biggie, but he gets a little befuddled beyond that.

His math lesson shows one of those complicated comma-laden, five-digit numbers: 13,209. Pointing to it, I ask, "How do you say that number?"

He ventures, "One trillion, three thousand..." and shakes his head, knowing that doesn't sound right. "I mean, one million, three thousand...two hundred nine...?" He raises his eyebrows at me in question.

I furrow my eyebrows back at him, and answer with as much seriousness as I can muster, "Close." For a seven year old, at least.

It's new and hard for him, and he needs encouragement. Grace. He's trying and he only needs a gentle correction for where he's at. Just like how God corrects us gently, because He knows where we're at, too.

Some seasons in life are hard, or confusing, or painfully dry, and He meets us where we are.

> *Preach the word; be ready in season and out of season; reprove, rebuke, and exhort, with complete patience and teaching.*
>
> *- 2 Timothy 4:2*

Some nights, this mama is squeezed dry from climbing hills of discipline and strife all day, and sliding back down again, over and over. When we barely skid to 8 pm, I don't feel warm, gentle, or full of grace.

On those days – you have them, too? – I shut their bedroom doors and collapse on the couch, depleted, but suddenly hear all sorts of whooping and revelry in the boys' room above me, where they're acting out some wild rumpus and I have to break up the party.

I'd love to tell you how it goes:

I put my Bible aside, sighing, and walk up the stairs. I open their door, and calmly – calmly, I tell you – remind them to be quiet. "This is Mama's rest time, Sweeties," *I croon,* "and you need to be in bed, reading or sleeping." *And, of course, they obey without hesitation as perfect little lambs, with no baaaahing or bleating for the rest of the night.*

It would be so awesome to tell you that. But I would be lying.

Because what really happens is ridiculous: I holler upstairs, hoping to somehow avoid having to get off the couch.

This never works. The fact that I still do it after thirteen years of parenting betrays my utterly misguided approach to the situation, because these kids are making way too much noise to hear me. And we all know that yelling *"BE QUIET!"* at the top of our lungs isn't the best way to, ahem, get our point across.

So I push my things aside, stomp upstairs – the one advantage of all their noise is that they can't hear me coming to bust them in the act – and fling open the door.

Behold: One child hangs upside down, monkey bar style from the side of the bunk bed. Another boy straddles two beds, paused in mid-leap. The smallest boy is giddy, enjoying the show, absorbing the example of his bigger brothers who know better – and this is what really goads me. *They know better.*

It's not just the boys – I know better, too, but here I am in all my fury. The riot in freeze-frame would be hysterical if I weren't seething. I turn off their light, assign extra chores for the morning, and huff downstairs. There is grumbling, hissing, and stomping, and I won't even mention how the boys responded.

Coasting on fumes to the couch, I'm emptied of answers and out of patience. And He's right there with me, of course – He's been right there all day long, but suddenly it's just us, minus the mayhem. He is never maddened or exhausted with my questions:

How do we go from the warmth of a happy afternoon to ending the day with a cold snap? Why must we close the day broken and angry and out of sorts, when all I want to do is tuck them in and finish strong? What happened?

Sometimes I'm the one who requires endless amounts of correction and teaching. He speaks, and the air around me starts to thaw.

Talk to Me, Love, He says. *Just like a little kid who talks to her parents incessantly, you need to talk to Me. I'm here to fill you all day long, because when you're hydrated with the Living Water, I can speak through you. You won't dry up, you won't get cold, and you'll never run on empty.*

He only calls us to speak to others the same way He speaks to us.

Put on then, as God's chosen ones, holy and beloved, compassionate hearts, kindness, humility, meekness, and patience.

- Colossians 3:12

If I could wrap my voice in this all the time as a salve for those who listen, the days would end warmly more often. Our fledglings would bud and blossom without drawing back in fear of frost. Little ears pay more attention to words swaddled in grace.

Don't forget to dress warmly, Love. Pray without ceasing, stay hydrated, and try again tomorrow.

And we do try again tomorrow, and every day after. I know better now, too.

It was a warm, grace-wrapped day when that four-year-old dumpling asked something serious. It was the Big Question.

"How do I give my heart to Jesus?" Oh, swooning bliss. Butterflies unwrapped their wings, trees burst into bloom, and birds sang the Hallelujah Chorus.

I composed myself, and said, "You tell Him you want to follow Him...that means you let Him be your boss."

She was incredulous. "He's gonna *boss* me?!"

"He's the nicest boss," I assured her. "If you don't know what to do, you can ask Him and He'll help you do the right thing."

"Oh," she said, with some relief.

"And...you know what? When you obey Him, I don't have to boss you so much." What a deal.

"Can I hear Him boss me?"

"Yep...you usually hear Him inside you. His voice is gentle. You recognize it with practice."

"Oh." Filled, warm, and happy with that little dose of theology, she ran off to play while I was still thinking of the words that just came out of my mouth. He uses these small ones to teach us so much.

Did you hear that? He said. My voice is gentle. You've learned to recognize it with practice. If you don't know what to do, ask Me…I'll help you do the right thing.

Stay close to Me. Blessed is the mama who delights in My law.

In every season, rain or shine, the mama who stays filled with Him keeps her home warm. She learns His voice. She points others to Him.

She stays wrapped in grace, and carries spring everywhere she goes.

Our home, like yours maybe, has several work stations. The dining table doubles as a school desk, an ancient sideboard holds our computer, and the kitchen is often on duty from nine in the morning to well past midnight. But there's one particular area that holds most of my affection – my family generously calls it "Mom's work table" although to be honest, there's almost no table to be seen underneath the mess of yarn and papers on top of it. Projects, craft stuff, books, a bazillion works in progress. Sometimes they even get finished.

But some days it all seems so trivial.

I get tired of the headlines. They are so big, and we are so small. We grieve and rage and share and pray and give money and still, the headlines keep coming, relentless.

What do we do in the face of such events? Disasters, persecution, and cruelty of epic proportions occurred throughout the centuries, but what makes our time period unique is that earlier generations never dealt with the onslaught of information overload of multiple tragedies occurring

simultaneously all over the world. We see photos, we hear about it every day on the news, in Facebook, in our email alerts. We are bombarded with appeals – mostly genuine, some not – to give, fund, call, sign, share, and do something about every single issue. Right now. Don't delay. Before it's too late. The times and the needs are urgent.
And they are. I know they are.

But I just can't. I can't do it all, sign it all, share it all, or fund it all, any more than I can answer the appeals from several of my kids banging on the bathroom door, asking for different things all at the same time while I'm still zipping my pants and haven't even flushed yet.

The noise is too much, and when it gets to a certain point I instinctively shut my eyes and cringe, the sound of blood rushing in my ears quieting everything else in self-defense. For the love of all that is holy, *one thing at a time.*

First, flush. Then maybe we can tackle the world, with all of its questions and conflicts.

I feel this constant pull in two directions. On one side is the simplicity of building a happy home and nurturing beauty in a quiet life, but on the other side is an urgent feeling of the critical times we live in and wanting to best prepare for it as a good steward of the King.

Maybe you're more balanced than I am, but I'm constantly asking Him questions like these:

When there are orphans needing families, people grieving, bodies hurting, and communities desperate for truth, why do I put so much time into the projects on my table? What good is reading, writing, rearranging bookshelves, or crocheting an afghan? Why should we spend time painting, or playing music, or, well, *steam cleaning the carpet* (if we're going to be really honest) when there is a culture to transform?

He answers, *Because there **is** a culture to transform, Love. That's exactly why. Your life and the details in it are a witness to others about My Kingdom. It's all ministry.*

He knows the joy in creating intricate detail, constructing beauty where before there was only ugliness and disorder.

> *Christianity alone has the resources to re-store the arts to their proper place, for Christianity is a worldview that supports human creativity yet does so with appro-priate humility. Made in the image of the Creator, humans find fulfillment in being creative in their own sphere. Yet unlike God, the human artist does not create out of nothing.*
>
> *- Charles Colson [3]*

The same God who loves the orphan and heals the dying is also the Designer concerned with the finest veins on a leaf, the stripes on a housecat, and the changes wrought in every season. He knows why we enjoy sewing stitches, composing music, and making paint strokes and key strokes.

We imitate our Father in the creator/designer aspect that is innovative and beautiful. We also reflect Him in the healer/redeemer role that is passionate, nurturing, world changing, and in the trenches.

And both sides are necessary. Too much time focused on aesthetics leaves us aloof and ignorant, and too much time entrenched in warfare leaves us burned out and bitter. But one more thing is needed to keep us in healthy equilibrium between the two, without which any light we attempt to create is blown out.

His presence is fire. Without it, no light. Our imitation of Him is only a puff of hot air if we aren't actually spending time with Him.

> *To work from large interests and a desire for great activity and world movements, to the inner circle life with Me, is really the wrong way. That is why so often, when...a soul finds Me, I have to begin our Friendship by cutting away the ties that bind it to the outer and wider circle. When it has gained strength and learned its lesson in the inner circle, it can then widen its life, working this time from within out, taking then to each contact, each friendship, the inner circle influence.*
>
> *And this is to be your way of life.*
>
> *This is the way of the Spirit.* 4

Hunkered down in His presence, our gifts press out and expand the Kingdom. We influence the culture through high quality works of excellence that command and deserve attention, *Soli Deo Gloria* style.

It is love that matters – the kind that moves, grows, and transforms. Love, focused. Love, unswerving. Love, triumphant.

> *Love one another with brotherly affection.*

Outdo one another in showing honor.

Do not be slothful in zeal, be fervent in the Spirit, serve the Lord.

Rejoice in hope, be patient in tribulation, be constant in prayer.

Contribute to the needs of the saints and seek to show hospitality.

- Romans 12:10-13

It is our time, on purpose, in His purpose. Just as we face bills and deadlines and diagnoses, the phone ringing and the toddler crying and the oven timer beeping. Just as we face oncoming vehicles on multiple lane highways, traffic lights, horns, sirens, and kids complaining from the backseat about the music on the radio – we're on information overload, but we've been trained to multi-task like no other culture.

We were made for this, in this time, perfectly.

It's not necessarily pretty – sometimes the stimuli stresses us out. We get grumpy, we yell things we probably shouldn't, and sometimes, yes, we forget to flush...but with a few exceptions, what needs to be done, gets done. What doesn't get done, you can maybe blame on the preschooler.

We were made for such a time as this, and not in the "each one of us has a small part to play" kind of role. Our impact is enormous. We face the news, we face the events, unswerving and unflinching in love that changes the headlines of tomorrow.

Each display of love, no matter how seemingly small, is a powerful act of spiritual

warfare that removes anxiety from the en-
vironment and replaces it with freedom
and safety.

– Danny Silk 5

Love, in kindness – it can change someone's day, which then changes their future.

Love, in righteous anger – quiet, self controlled, and motivating.

Love, in education – refusing to give in to apathy, ignorance, or laziness. We are not those who shrink back.

Love, in generosity – because He has modeled extravagance to us.

Love, in hope – not wishful thinking, but confident knowing and patient creativity.

Love, in prayer – above all else, unceasing, relentless, and effective.

Love, in worship – because we know Who we are dealing with.

The distractions buzz around a wind-smeared August sky, creating more noise. In the rapidly waning summer, I removed commitments my heart was no longer fully behind, because those endeavors were a burden no longer authorized by the Spirit and I let go of them in order to walk through the threshold. *All things are lawful, but not all things build up* – and this is a time that requires building.

Each gift used from His presence is a fire, full of grace and beauty, yet uncompromising in truth. Our culture sees Him by the light of it and is transformed.

*For while we were still weak, at the right
time Christ died for the ungodly.*

- Romans 5:6

He was right on time. And we will arrive at our
destination, on time, too.

*Do not be overcome by evil, but overcome
evil with good.*

- Romans 12:21

We walk the path He calls us to – signing,
singing, going, giving, praying, trusting, hoping,
doing, waiting, sharing, learning, growing.
    Persevering. Love, triumphant. For the love of
all that is holy.

From my spot on the couch in the living room I
can see Vin in the kitchen, slightly hunched,
peering at something. It takes me a second to
realize what he's doing.
    "You look like you've seen a mosquito."
    "I did. I'm tracking him." The fearless hunter
grabs a child's pinwheel off the counter, wields it
like a flyswatter, and nails that sucker.
    Always, always, the mosquitoes. They are ob-
noxious, humbling creatures, buzzing through
every activity while we enjoy our backyard bar-
becues, harvest parties, and 2 am sunsets.
    Alaska doesn't sleep in the summer. It's not the
noise, though, or even the mosquitoes; it's the
daylight. May through August, it's unceasing except

for a brief nap in the wee hours, when it just barely gets tucked in before coming out again like a toddler who's had too much sugar.

Our summers are short but we pack a lot into them. By fall, the fair is crowded with samples of the most abundant, wow-normous veggies you've ever seen. But it's mostly just good soil combined with never-sleeping sun.

> *As for what was sown on good soil, this is the one who hears the word and understands it. He indeed bears fruit and yields, in one case a hundredfold, in another sixty, and in another thirty.*
>
> *– Matthew 13:23*

And we are His dust, partnered with Daylight. The harvest comes from His presence in us, never sleeping.

There's a time and a place for loud declarations, but most of our influence – the fruit we bear – comes from the quiet, persistent attendance of Jesus in every area of our lives. Not by painting crosses on everything we make, but by pursuing the giftings and talents He created us with and then using them boldly, wisely, and well in every sphere He puts us.

> *What we want is not more little books about Christianity, but more little books by Christians on other subjects – with their Christianity latent.*
>
> *– C.S. Lewis* [6]

It's Christianity that is not shushed or hidden, but inherent. It's Jesus permeating everything through His people, even on a cloudy day when sin and mosquitoes are everywhere discouraging us.

He's leaving no stone unturned in the tilling as we partner with Him in the harvest. And we bear healthier fruit when we enrich our soil – filling ourselves with His words and educating ourselves with great works of His people. We're not looking for just anything we can get our hands on; we're using our time and resources strategically to guard and prepare our hearts. We want a vast array of nourishing, challenging, truth-filled content that grows and inspires us.

Keep your heart with all vigilance, for from it flows the springs of life.

– Proverbs 4:23

But we also need rest. Like soil, we need downtime or we get depleted and nothing can grow from us. We need firm boundaries from buzzing negativity that harasses and discourages us. We need dates with our spouse, Sabbaths, and occasional afternoon breaks behind a locked door with a clandestine bar of chocolate that isn't shared with the kids. At least, I do.

And He said to them, "Come away by yourselves to a desolate place and rest a while." For many were coming and going, and they had no leisure even to eat.

– Mark 6:31

We're meant to bear exceptional fruit, not just low-quality filler taking up space and adding to the noise. We're made to pour out our gifts in a way that reflects the excellent nature of the original Creator – generously, without fear, and trusting Him with the results. When we do, it creates a culture that can't ignore the Light permeating it.

The good person out of the good treasure of his heart produces good, and the evil person out of his evil treasure produces evil, for out of the abundance of the heart his mouth speaks.

– Luke 6:45

It looks like a woman quietly honing her craft, praying for each recipient, praying for every city and town her products are sent to – calmly, discreetly, silently brightening the future of everyone she comes in contact with.

It looks like a man working, teaching, leading in integrity and purity, steadfast in the place God has him. Co-workers notice the wisdom there; relationships and trust build. Joy, grace, and truth grow in the community.

It looks like families soaring through sunshine but also plodding and persevering through dark nights. Sons watch the devotion of their father and learn how to be a husband and provider for their future wife, while she is still in pigtails. Daughters watch their mamas on good days and hard days, and learn how to nurture generations yet unborn.

Their soil is rich, their harvest is abundant. *That is influence.*

How could any good thing happen in a fallen world without the grace of God and the prayers of His people? We get our hands dirty and take His daylight everywhere we go, in both the frenzied sleepless activity and the restful, lazy breezes.

And then we crush the mosquitoes – oh, yes we do! – and toss them in the dirt pile. But nothing is wasted. The harassment turns into compost, and it enriches our soil, too.

I'm not sure how many hours of my life I've spent typing away at the computer, but I do know that I waste a lot of that time by peeking at the keyboard, checking on and doubting my progress. When I'm paying too much attention to the process, typos are everywhere.

Shoot, was that really where the P was? And did I hit the semicolon, or the apostrophe? I go back to check and lose time in a series of backspacing, retyping, and hitting the "undo" button.

But when I don't constantly look at the keyboard, I make very few errors. When I'm pounding away blindly at the keys and finally review the screen to check it all, I'm amazed at the lack of typos. It stuns me every time. I really do know what I'm doing, as long as I'm not second guessing too much.

But I tend to second guess a lot of things. The mission is hard. Some stuff looks like it's not working out, and other situations look like they're falling apart entirely. Do you feel this, friends?

Likewise the Spirit helps us in our weak-

ness. For we do not know what to pray for as we ought, but the Spirit himself intercedes for us with groanings too deep for words. And he who searches hearts knows what is the mind of the Spirit, because the Spirit intercedes for the saints according to the will of God.

– Romans 8:26-27

We chant this refrain of, *God, what have we done? If we were doing it right, surely it would be working...we must be doing something wrong... should I hit the undo button? Or should I just highlight the whole shebang and hit delete?*

I check, and look, and doubt progress, forgetting that completing the work takes a million keystrokes. Much is happening under the surface.

*And the Lord said to Joshua, "See, **I have given Jericho into your hand**, with its king and mighty men of valor. **You shall march around the city**, all the men of war going around the city once. **Thus shall you do for six days.** Seven priests shall bear seven trumpets of rams' horns before the ark. **On the seventh day you shall march around the city seven times**, and the priests shall blow the trumpets.*

– Joshua 6:2-4

The instructions are specific. We know which direction we're going and what we're supposed to do once we get there. So why isn't it working?

Stop counting steps, He tells me. *Just count the laps and don't overthink it. The truth is, Love, that wall is coming down – it's just that you've only walked around it three or four times.*

> *Enemy-occupied territory – that is what this world is. Christianity is the story of how the rightful king has landed, you might say landed in disguise, and is calling us all to take part in a great campaign of sabotage.*
>
> – C.S. Lewis [7]

If we are in obedience and things still seem to be falling apart, we might be right where He wants us: heavily engaged, typing away, focused on the mission at hand, not missing the forest for the trees. Those on the front lines come under the heaviest fire, and each of our positions is a strategic assignment.

> *And at the seventh time, when the priests had blown the trumpets, Joshua said to the people, "Shout, for the Lord has given you the city."*
>
> – Joshua 6:16

Our obedience – steadfast, unwavering, swerving neither to the right nor left – is one of the greatest threats to the enemy. Combined with worship, it liberates captives and takes the city.

The kettle sings, the tea steeps.

After a stinky day, I feel heavy and burdened and I don't want to write about it. Grumbling and sulking, I lift out the teabag and stir in cream. Toss the spoon on the counter. Flop onto the couch. I am in my late thirties, going on fourteen and self-pity.

Just write anyway, He says. *Someone else feels heavy, too.*

The kids are in bed, the white cat is on my feet, and I'm listening. He speaks:

This day does not define you. The questions, assumptions, and judgments of others do not define you. Your children's behavior does not define you.

What about...?

Nope. Not your biological kids, either.

Even when their behavior is a reflection of yours – whether good or bad – it doesn't define who you are. I'm moving in every part of this. Not a moment, not a situation is wasted.

Do you remember a year ago?

And I answer, Must I? Do I really have to?

I know. Some things were better. Most were much more difficult.

Those things that you are discouraged by, those things that seem to be in limbo with no progress, only seem the same on the surface. They are about to transform like a rapidly blooming desert flower that will remain unfading because My work is everlasting in you and in those you love.

You need to do more than picture the victory now, Love. You need to expect it.

These days of listening for Him are like gathering manna – knowing that I have no words without

His provision, but trusting Him to lay the pieces out for me every day to find and pick up. And He always does. They're not always where I think they are; sometimes they take longer to put together than I'd like. We all want answers for our questions...but we also want to have a say in the answers we get.

Sometimes He's the one gathering up the pieces for us. Sometimes we fall into pieces from the happenings of the day, the test results, the phone call, and He pulls us together again, taking every scheme of the enemy and turning it on its head for our good, and His goodness.

And we know that for those who love God
all things work together for good, for those
who are called according to his purpose.

– Romans 8:28

These days, though – sometimes they just strip us. We're riddled with holes, events chipping away at us, our pieces strewn everywhere – we gather them up, try to fit them back together, but it's not happening. Too many mistakes. Too much brokenness.

They don't fit together; they're not made to go together. No matter which way we turn them, all we have is a mess *because those pieces were meant to be taken out.*

The pieces aren't the real picture; the real work of art is what's left when the pieces are removed, like a sculpture, or paper snowflake, or an excavated treasure.

He picks up our pieces and gives them back to us, but they will be transformed, and so will we.

He'll say, *This peace is for you. And in this hurtful situation, this peace is for you. And this act of forgiveness, and this gesture of kindness, and all of these moves in obedience...they are for you, too.* **This peace is for you.**

The real masterpiece is His child, refined though maturity and surrender. His people, trained for battle and victory.

We see it in Joshua. A grave mistake was made in the first battle after Jericho – one man sinned, the entire nation lost the battle of Ai, and it was a devastating follow-up to what looked so promising after the victory at Jericho.

And yet, God. They dealt with the sin, and God sent them back to Ai. He turned the failure on its head and used it for good:

> *[Joshua said] "And I and all the people who are with me will approach the city. And when they come out against us just as before, we shall flee before them. And they will come out after us, until we have drawn them away from the city. For* ***they will say, 'They are fleeing from us, just as before.'*** *So we will flee before them.* ***Then you shall rise up from the ambush and seize the city, for the Lord your God will give it into your hand.***"

– Joshua 8:5-7

They did the hard work of repentance and obedience, and then they went back and won the city. And they won the next one, and the next one, and then a foreign king tried to help another city against Joshua and the Israelites, but that was a terrible idea because they beat him, too. On and on, until they cleared Canaan, north and south. *Shout, for the Lord has given you the city...* They wiped the giants from the land.

I typed out the words "September newsletter" for my subscribers and I'm not sure how we got here already. And what's more, if I'm typing those words it means we're not just touching September, but plowing most of the way through it. Winter is already waving at us from the next page over.

But however it happened, fall is here again in all its glory – the sunlight streams through birch trees and leaves tumble in gusts of wind. And it's not just leaves, but the angle of light showed something else that looked like sawdust – the tiny birch seeds were flying, too. They are light flecks, shaped like a cross, a plus sign, or birds in flight.

Fall is for newness. More than spring, more than the New Year, fall to me has always been about beginnings. September signals the time for new classes, new teachers, new friends, new pencils, new endeavors.

Spring and summer are prelude. Or as Vince says, they are the stretching before the real game begins. Fall is when things really start to happen, as we get ready for the high noon of deep winter in Alaska.

We took advantage of the weather and drove to the hike I grew up on, just a little mountain in the middle of a one-light town. We parked the Stagecoach, put the honor system fee in the slot, and headed up.

The first few minutes are steep, and I stopped every few minutes to gasp for breath under the guise of taking photos. We hadn't hiked this trail in years, so I was enthralled and had a lot of opportunities to catch my breath and take pictures. One hundred forty-four photos...not exaggerating. I really love to breathe.

Skeletons of cow parsnip stood above still-green nettle along the dusty trail of hard-packed silt. Cham kept trying to write her name in it, though the footsteps of every hiker following the common path near the bottom of the trail made it impossible. Also, every grain of loose dirt had already been picked up by Reagan, who took a tumble down the hill backwards while I was gawking at horses and taking pictures.

We also saw three eagles – birds in flight, shaped like birch seeds, a cross, a plus sign.

The shades of green are lush and magical; we could be in England, we could be in Ireland, we could be in Middle Earth. But there were unique moments that were distinctly American, too, like when my romantic thoughts were broken in by my husband calling up the hillside to Afton, "Crouch like you're holding a rifle! Yell, 'Wolverines!'"

There was also an unmistakably Alaskan moment on the way down, when I pointed out the reindeer in the farm below us. Cham said, "You mean, the animals that – " and, silly me, I thought she was going to say something about Santa, or Christmas, or the like. But no, not at all.

"You mean the animals that we eat in reindeer sausage?" she asked.

Yes, dear. Those ones.

She kept trying to write in the dirt, and finally, nearer the top, off the main part of the trail, the ground was soft enough.

And it is this way God writes His name in us – in the good soil, away from the common path where the dirt is hardened beyond His impression. It only happens farther up the mountain.

Winter is coming...so up we go. Out of the common, out of the prelude, away from the clean comfort zone we're used to, where we can get our hands dirty. When people see us, they will know we've encountered Him. They will see His name written in our hearts, as we pray and change the future through conversation with the One who holds it all.

Notes

Chapter 1: Abiding

1. Brother Lawrence, *The Practice of the Presence of God* (Peabody, Mass: Hendrickson Publishers, 2004), 22.

2. Ibid, 47.

3. Ibid, 47-48.

4. *God Calling*, ed. A.J. Russell (Ulrichsville, Ohio: Barbour Publishing, 1998), entry titled "February 11."

Chapter 2: Identity

1. Madeleine L'Engle, *A Circle of Quiet* (San Francisco: HarperCollins, 1972), 233.

2. Daniel Defoe, *Robinson Crusoe* (London: Penguin Books, 2003), 14-15.

3. Jerry Bridges, *The Pursuit of Holiness* (Colorado Springs: NavPress, 2006), 80.

Chapter 3: Threshold

1. John Bunyan, *Pilgrim's Progress* (New York: Grosset & Dunlap, no year listed), 251.

2. Brother Lawrence, *The Practice of the Presence of God* (Peabody, Mass: Hendrickson Publishers, 2004), 38.

3. Ibid, 38-39.

4. Ibid, 39.

5. C.S. Lewis, *Mere Christianity* (New York: MacMillan Publishing Company, 1952), 44-45.

6. Stephen Mansfield, *Never Give In: The Extraordinary Character of Winston Churchill* (Nashville: Cumberland House Publishing, 1995), 209-210.

Chapter 4: Forward

1. C.S. Lewis, *The Horse and His Boy* (New York: HarperCollins, 1954), 190.

Chapter 5: Friendship

1. William Goldman, *The Princess Bride* (Cutchogue, NY: Buccaneer Books, 1973), 283-284.

2. Stephen Mansfield, *Never Give In: The Extraordinary Character of Winston Churchill* (Nashville: Cumberland House Publishing, 1995), 54.

3. Kenneth Grahame, *The Wind in the Willows* (New York: Sterling Publishing Co., 2005), 48.

4. Ibid, 74.

Chapter 6: Fire

1. See Matthew 18:19, Matthew 21:22, Mark 11:24, John 14:13, John 15:7, John 15:16, John 16:23-24, James 1:5-6, James 1:17, 1 John 3:22, and 1 John 5:14-15.

2. Victor Hugo, *Les Miserables* (New York: Fall River Press, 2012), 790.

3. Ibid.

4. Ibid.

5. C.S. Lewis, *Mere Christianity* (New York: MacMillan Publishing Company, 1952), 147.

Chapter 7: Light

1. Charles Colson, *How Now Shall We Live?* (Wheaton, Ill: Tyndale Publishers, 1999), 450.

2. *God Calling*, ed. A.J. Russell (Ulrichsville, Ohio: Barbour Publishing, 1998), entry titled "February 14."

3. Charles Colson, *How Now Shall We Live?* (Wheaton, Ill: Tyndale Publishers, 1999), 449.

4. *God Calling*, ed. A.J. Russell (Ulrichsville, Ohio: Barbour Publishing, 1998), entry titled "November 28."

5. Danny Silk, *Keep Your Love On* (Redding, Calif: Keep Your Love On, 2013).

6. C.S. Lewis, *The Collected Works of C.S. Lewis*, from the essay "Christian Apologetics" (New York: Inspirational Press, 1996), 362.

7. C.S. Lewis, *Mere Christianity* (New York: MacMillan Publishing Company, 1952), 51.

Acknowledgments

Deepest thanks to...

God the Father, Son, and Spirit, Who calls me after His own name.

Vince, who went wild and quit his job so we could live the dream, and still stuck with it even when the dream meant doing terrible things like learning html, coding, and avoiding the use of too many adverbs. I think it's so sexy when you fix formatting and tweak web design.

Our kids, who were (mostly) enthusiastic about this project, even if it was because we promised them a kitten (or was it chickens?) and who cooked meals and did school and took care of the Littles to help make it happen. Thank you for not asking for a pony. (No. Just no, don't even think about it.)

My close friends and pastors who reviewed and critiqued the manuscript before it was pretty, and also put up with all of my nosy questions: Leslie Cotton, Lenora Brake, Arianne Herglotz, and Cindy Epperson. You guys embody the friendship chapter, and each of you is a force to be reckoned with.

Kelly Bermudez, who navigated dozens of texts and emails to do the artwork for the cover. His gift in you is a gift to me and everyone else who sees your work.

The following loved ones who, while not directly involved in the creative process, were greatly involved in my heart process while writing this book: Jess, who nurtured and prayed from a dis-tance, even though I am a terrible correspondent; Wendy, who provided much of the material for the friendship chapter (and is a keeper); Amanda, with whom I've walked an eerily parallel journey for 17 years running and will always be one of my favorites; my three amigos in the Fab Four, Robin, Maggie, and Jenna, whose E/INFPness brings great levity to my INTJness; Trudy, who is the best neighbor-tutor-pastor-boss-friend-piano teacher our crazy family could ask for; Larry and Sharon, Cody and Sara, and Joel and Sonya, who have walked so many miles with us that they've become family to us; and Grandma and Dad, who always supported me and seemed to think I could do this, and didn't act too surprised when I finally did.

My readers, whose comments, emails, messages, and encouragement make my day. I'm so honored every time you invite my words into your inbox, screens, and bookshelves. Thank you for learning with me.

One more thing...

Do you want more encouragement in the season you're in? Do you want to grow deep and wide, regardless of your space and circumstances?

You are warmly invited to copperlightwood.com where we're transparent about finding peace in the hard moments, beauty in the mess, and white space in the chaos. It's a little unpolished here, so watch out for the Legos on the floor.

His peace is for you,

Shannon Guerra

subscribe:

eepurl.com/MugpP

connect:

instagram.com/copperlightwood
facebook.com/copperlightwood
goodreads.com/shannonguerra